Guerrilla Marketing For Real Estate Investors:

101 Ways To Market Your Business

MARK EVANS, DM
& JAY CONRAD LEVINSON

DM Publishing
Deal Maker Publishing, LLC

Guerrilla Marketing For Real Estate Investors
101 Ways To Market Your Business™

ISBN #: 9780978817022

Printed in the United States of America
This publication is designed to provide competent and reliable information regarding the subject matters covered. However, it is sold with the understanding that the author and publisher are not engaged in rendering legal, financial, or other professional advice. If legal or other expert assistance is required, the services of a professional should be sought. The author and publisher specifically disclaim any liability that is incurred from the use or application of the contents of this book.

All companies and domains are registered trademarks of their respective companies and we are, in no way, shape, or form, endorsed or affiliated with any company.

Please visit our website at
www.MarkEvansDM.com

The author and publisher would like to acknowledge and thank the participants in this book who have granted us permission to cite their trademarked and copyrighted materials and publications.

Table of Contents

Dedication

This book is dedicated to you, the reader. Without you, the words are merely words. But when you implement these words in your business, you will grow a real estate business that most will only dream of; you will succeed at the highest levels. So I dedicate this book to all those who will take this book and run with what they learn here.

My main word to you? It's simple, but not always easy: Go for your dreams! More importantly, *live your dreams.*

&&&

To my grandmother and grandfather, Ben and Reah Evans who allowed and encouraged me to ask a million questions a day. Thanks for being awesome grandparents.

&&&

To my parents who are the *best* parents in the world and who have and will always be there to offer me guidance and support. Thanks for showing up at my sporting events all of those years. If you only knew how much that meant then, and still means to me yet today. Thank you for being so selfless and giving me more then any kid could ever imagine.

About the Author

Mark Evans, DM, is a full-time world traveler and full-time virtual real estate investor. He is a master at creating multiple streams of income and is a life-long student of marketing. As such, he has turned his attention toward reaching out to others to teach them how to live life on their terms.

Mark has developed many groundbreaking online systems and best-selling real estate products. These online tools allow investors to easily create multiple streams of income online in their sleep. Not only is Mark a real estate investor but he has subsequently become a successful real estate investing coach, and has students all around the world. He gets excited about helping others who are ready and willing to help themselves! His willingness to help is more than just words—Mark offers simple but powerful instruction, guidance and direction through his many programs.

This three-time best-selling author (with many more to come) has a passion and a zest for life that is infectious. This zeal for life and reaching out is reflected in the fact that he donates book sale percentages to many well-deserving charitable foundations. These philanthropic endeavors help those less fortunate. Says Mark, “We can always do more by helping others to achieve their goals.”

By achieving all of this (and more!), Mark Evans, DM, truly does live up to his title of Deal Maker.

Jay Conrad Levinson is the author of the best-selling marketing series in history, *Guerrilla Marketing*, plus 59 other business books. His books have sold more than 21-million copies worldwide. His guerrilla concepts have influenced marketing so much that his books appear in 62 languages and are required reading in MBA programs across the globe.

He was born in Detroit, raised in Chicago, and graduated from the University of Colorado. His studies in Psychology led him to advertising agencies, including a Directorship at Leo Burnett in London, where he served as Creative Director. Upon his return to the US, he joined J. Walter Thompson as Senior VP. Jay created and taught guerrilla marketing for ten years at the extension division of the University of California in Berkeley.

A winner of first prizes in all the media, he has been part of the creative teams that made household names of The Marlboro Man, The Pillsbury Doughboy, Allstate's good hands, United's friendly skies, Sears' Diehard battery, Morris the Cat, Mr. Clean, Tony the Tiger, and the Jolly Green Giant.

Today, *Guerrilla Marketing* is most the powerful brand in the history of marketing, listed among the 100 best business books ever written, a popular website at www.gmarketing.com, and powers The Guerrilla Marketing Association, a support system for small business.

After living in the San Francisco Bay Area for 35 years, Jay and Jeannie Levinson sold their home, bought an RV, towed a Jeep, and ended up, six years later, at their lakefront home outside Orlando,

Florida, and close to their 26 grandchildren—their own personal Disney World. Nobody on earth is as qualified to write about Guerrilla Marketing than the Father of Guerrilla Marketing, Jay Conrad Levinson.

Author Notes

- **Do you want more buyers for your real estate deals?**
- **Do you want to get more money to do more deals?**
- **Do you want to get that money without having to qualify?**
- **Do you want to be able to work less and make more money?**

Throughout this book, you are going to be handed some of the simplest and most powerful ways to gain instant credibility. You will learn how to acquire more clients in *minutes*, not days, and you will learn how to accomplish these marketing strategies using little or none of your own cash.

The goal with this book is to give you insight into the truth about marketing. Simply put, it's all about perception and not about who you are or where you are at the time of marketing. Obviously, you will offer fair properties backed up with your personal morals and set of values. You will be a businessperson of integrity whose word can be counted on and trusted. Ideally, these foundational basics should go without saying and should apply to all business endeavors.

With regard to the real estate investment industry, I know that there are many great and talented people involved in this business wondering how they're going to eat today. Their businesses have hit the skids! Why? Because they have yet to grasp the fact that first and foremost, they are *marketers*.

Believe me when I say that this book is going to challenge your beliefs about what you are capable of accomplishing! Also believe me when I say you are just one great marketing campaign away from knocking it out of the ballpark. But—and this is a biggie—I warn you that not all marketing is created equal; nor is this simply a process of "market and make money." Not by a long shot. Realizing you are a marketer is just the first step in getting to the next level of achieving all that you have ever dreamed of.

This book is specifically designed to give you guidance and direction in marketing; it is not a book about business development. I am going to teach you fresh ideas, perspectives, and strategies. I want to arm you with the knowledge that will transform you into a force to be reckoned with.

This book is designed to teach you to draw more buyers for your real estate deals, attract more sellers who will come to you with their deals, and (this is my all-time favorite) create a lineup of investors who are waiting to not only purchase multiple deals from you, but to also come to you with their deals.

How to Use This Book

It was never my intent to simply create a book that contained a long list of resources. It should be apparent to the reader that some of the categories will offer many resources, while other categories offer something entirely different. And while some categories need extensive direction and explanation (such as video marketing) other categories need very little explanation (such as placing ads).

This is not a "read-through-once-and-you're-done" type of book. It is a "keep-at-your-fingertips-for-continual-reference" type of book. You will want to keep it where you can refer to it often.

Also, it is not even suggested that all of these resources must be in place in order for your business to be successful. Actually, there are probably a number of marketing strategies listed here that you're already using. My suggestion is that you select four or five techniques that seem to fit well into your existing business and begin to implement them. You should begin to incorporate more strategies into your marketing plan only after you've learned how to tweak those first four or five for the best results.

So here you are—you have been handed the golden keys to the fastest, easiest ways to generate more leads for your real estate business and make more money while working less. If that really gets your blood pumping and your heart pounding, then let's get started building your business and growing your real estate investing empire.

Chapter 1:
Fifteen Minutes a Day

Keep Up With Change

If you've been in the business of real estate investing for any time at all, you've seen a number of changes in our industry. Some investors have kept up with the changes, while others have been left in the dust. In this chapter, we'll talk about why that is and how these changes can affect you personally.

Obviously, the present economy has brought about monumental changes. Everyone in America and around the globe has seen and recognized these changes. While those economical changes are incredibly massive, the changes I'm talking about are greater and ultimately have more impact than what's going on with the economy. The changes I refer to are those that pertain to technology and the Internet.

In times past, a real estate investor could put a sign up on a pole and stick an ad in the local paper and the calls would just come flooding in. Those methods were perfectly effective for that time and era, but those days are long gone. Everything has changed. The "old school" ways of thinking, working, and marketing no longer work in today's high tech environment.

Research in the field shows that least 80% of home searches begin online, according to Realtor.com and www.TheMoveChannel.com. Today, when people want to look for houses to purchase, or for a way to get rid of unwanted properties, their first course of action is to immediately sit down at the computer and run searches on various search engines such as Google, Bing, and Yahoo! to name a few. And when they do, will they find you? If your answer is *no*, then this book is definitely for you. And, if you answered *yes,* then congrats, because this book is for you as well.

Be Equipped and Enabled

This book will take you on a journey through a variety of marketing resources. It is designed to put resources at your fingertips and to equip and enable you to become more productive, more effective, and more successful. You will learn about both online and offline resources, because both work together and both should be used.

Every resource in this book is designed with one major goal in mind, and that is to keep a continual flow of leads coming into your marketing system. Once you have that continuous flow, the next step is for you to be equipped to handle those leads through an automated system that will not demand your constant attention. In essence, it is designed to help your business become a hands-free operation.

Make Time for Yourself

It's a known fact that entrepreneurs, by nature, are *doers*! They like to live with their fingers in every pie. (Can you relate?) These qualities that lead you to be constantly moving, constantly working, are great to get your business up and going; long-term, however, they can be highly detrimental to your health and your life. You must always remember why you started your own investing business. Was it so you could trade one job for another? So you could work for long hours and still have no time for yourself or your family? Probably not.

You probably started your own business in order to create a lifestyle where your time was your own. Where you could set your own schedule and name your own hours. So, let me ask you: Has that happened yet? And, if it hasn't, are you setting things in motion to make it happen? Are you ready to?

I talk to real estate investors all across this country on a regular basis, and I can tell you that the majority are slaves to their businesses. Their time is absolutely and completely *not* their own. That's why this book came into being. It is to equip you as an investor to break free of thinking that everything depends on you, or that you *must* be in control of everything all the time. It's time to change your thinking; it's time to be set free.

This book is jam-packed full of information and resources that will work wonders for your business. However, remember that its success does not depend solely on you doing all the work. Nearly every strategy listed in this book can in some way be *outsourced.* And in case you thought outsourcing was just for huge corporations, you are in for a pleasant surprise (see Chapter 10).

I always advise investors beginning to implement new marketing strategies that they to do it themselves for few weeks. That way they become familiar with how it works and how it should be done. After that, they need to find a way get it off their plates as quickly as possible. Find some way to outsource each task.

Summary

If you consistently stick to this plan, eventually you will have a business that gives you the lifestyle you've always dreamed about. Your goal should be to get your business to the point where it takes about *fifteen minutes* a day to maintain. Think for a moment how stress-free your life would be if it required only fifteen minutes of your time each day! This isn't some far-fetched dream; this *is* possible.

Chapter 2:
What Business Are You In?

Be a Marketer First

I have had the privilege of working with many real estate investors from all parts of the country—and around the world! One of the most basic problems I encounter when listening to these investors is their lack of understanding exactly which business they are in!

You may be thinking that's a pretty simple question to answer: "What business are you in?" Naturally, if you are a real estate investor, you are in the real estate investing business, right? Wrong!

The truth of the matter is that you must become a *marketer first*! This seems to be the missing piece of the puzzle for so many investors. In fact, I am writing this book because of that very reason. Once you understand this basic truth—once you find this missing puzzle piece—you can become whatever you want and you can have whatever you want.

You have your own personal dreams and goals. There are places you want to go, things you want to do, things you want to have. You want to have the quality time to spend doing the things you love; you want time to spend with your family. Knowledge and understanding of the basic skills of marketing can help you achieve your dreams.

Think about this. No matter what business you happen to be in, you want and need buyers. And buyers are attracted only through effective marketing.

Make Marketing Primary

Now you know you must become an effective marketer before you can become an effective real estate investor. As this truth begins to soak in, you will come to realize that as far as business goes, without marketing you have nothing.

In this simple but powerful book you will be introduced to many different ways to market your real estate investing business. Some of these strategies are absolutely free! Others are of minimal cost. Still others require a larger cash outlay. Think of how easy it will be to begin with *free* resources, and then move up as your cash flow increases.

The goal is not for you to implement all of the resources listed in this book at the same time. That would be impossible, and it would likely land you in the loony bin very quickly. You know your own talents, your resources, and your present cash flow. As you read through these ideas, you should choose perhaps four or five marketing techniques that fit in your business, and into your lifestyle. And then implement them as fast as possible.

Create Momentum

There is much to be said for momentum, and that's why it's important to begin implementing your strategies as soon as you can. Marketing is like the proverbial snowball. It may take a little huffing and puffing for you to get that snowball to the brow of the hill, but once it starts down the other side—look out! Not only will it move faster and faster, it will grow as well.

These ideas and strategies are designed to provide you with the knowledge of where to market along with action plans to help you implement them.

Create Your Marketing Funnel

Before we get into the broader subject of marketing, I want to cover one crucial issue. Regarding your online presence, it is imperative that you have more than one Squeeze Page to act as your marketing funnel. This is how to attract different prospects to your business. Let's look closer as to why multiple Squeeze Pages are so important.

I think you will agree that buyers' needs are different from the needs of sellers, and that investors have different needs than buyers and sellers.

For instance, when someone is trying to sell a house, they are not looking for information on the best way to get financing. A potential home seller wants to know the quickest and easiest way to move that house. A similar principle applies to buyers; they have their own particular set of needs. Buyers want to know about all the different financing options that are available to them. Obviously, they don't need to learn about the "Seven Steps to Selling Your Home."

Investors have a totally different mindset. They want to learn about ways to get discounts on properties and they want to know who can supply them with choice deals. Unlike the general buyers and sellers, investors are most always repeat customers. They will be doing a high volume of business on an ongoing basis. You want to offer them exactly what they are looking for.

This concept is very easy to understand and actually pretty easy to implement; however, so many investors try to make "one size fit all." They try to fit everyone's needs into one website with the thought that this will save money. In truth they lose money by not targeting Squeeze Pages to the proper audiences.

It's a fact that many real estate investors aren't up with the latest technology. Technology is just usually not their forte. The truth is, one doesn't necessarily have to be a computer geek to tap into the resources available. It is relatively simple to create multiple squeeze pages. It comes with an awareness of how important this step is in the development of your key marketing strategies. This can happen with a couple clicks of a mouse and for less than a cup of coffee a day. (See Chapter 5 for more information about Squeeze Pages, which are simple online pages whose only objective is to "squeeze" names and E-mail addresses from potential prospects in exchange for more information.)

Summary

Know what business you are in. Grasp the fact that no business can survive without effective marketing. First of all, learn to market, then implement effective marketing techniques such as those featured in this book, and your success is assured.

Chapter 3:
The Secret to Creating Strong Classifieds

Marketing Resource #1: www.CraigsList.com *

Craig's List is by far one of your best, quickest, and easiest (no cost) advertising mediums online. The key to success on Craig's List is to stay at the top of the listings. This is the way to get the best traffic. To stay at the top, simply re-post your listings periodically. You will need to create several versions of your ad, as Craig's List does not accept duplicate postings. Also note that Craig's List allows photos.

Occasionally, Craig's List may delete your ads. Don't let that deter you.

Marketing Resource #2: www.BackPage.com *

Marketing Resource #3: www.Kijiji.com *

Marketing Resource #4: www.USFreeAds.com *

Marketing Resource #5: www.ClassifiedAds.com*

Marketing Resource #6: www.USNetAds.com *

Marketing Resource #7: www.Oodle.com *

Marketing Resource #8: www.DomesticSale.com*

Marketing Resource #9: www.Geebo.com *

Marketing Resource #10: www.OLX.com *

Marketing Resource #11: www.Upillar.com *

Marketing Resource #12: www.SaleSpider.com *

**** Ad services are free of cost***

Understand Classifieds as a Marketing Mainstay

Classified ads have been the backbone for many real estate investors' marketing plans. They are both simple and effective. Classifieds cannot only announce your properties in print publications, but they also work in cyberspace.

When talking about classifieds, we are differentiating from sites that allow you to post your available properties complete with an array of photos and a complete descriptions. Online classified ads are very short—like the ones you find at the back of a newspaper.

I have talked to many investors who are unaware of the many online classified sites that are available. This is a shame because, unlike your local newspaper, the use of these sources is often completely cost-free. Once you become aware of such an opportunity, how could you pass it up?

When you post a classified ad, you're competing with dozens of other ads. Because of that, you must know how to make the most of this strategy. In this chapter, we'll cover a number of tips, ideas, and how-to's, which will keep you way ahead of the competition, and draw an abundance of leads to your business.

Check Your Competition

Before posting an ad anywhere, spend a little time reading the ad areas you plan to target. Look for ads offering similar products or services, and think about how you can present your case in a more compelling way.

Use a Strong Title

Your classified ad is nothing more than a title in a list of titles until someone opens it and reads it. The title is the only way to get people interested enough to find out what you have to say, so you have to make it count. Create a title of about 40 characters or less. Ad titles longer than this may not be completely displayed on the screen.

I see lots of ads with vague titles like "More Income Now!" or "Free Information Kit." Titles like "Creative Financing for your Next House," or "Free Report: How to Sell Your House Fast" are better. Be specific.

Use Power Words

Every professional advertiser knows that words like "free," "secret," "money," "guarantee," "earn," and "save" push people's buttons and make them want to hear more. Become a student of print advertising headlines and learn how to use power words in your own ad titles (See Sidebar "The Magic and Tragic Words of Marketing").

Don't Shout

Ad titles that are printed with all capital letters or which contain lots of asterisks, exclamation points, dollar signs, or other keyboard symbols are the online equivalent of shouting or using tacky flashing neon signs. They say to your audience that you're not smart or professional enough to write an effective ad title, so you're trying to get their attention by shouting instead.

Make Your Message Complete but Concise

Your reader's patience (and time) is severely limited, so craft your advertising message carefully to explain:

A) What you're offering

B) Why the reader might want it, and

C) What they should do to get it.

The trick is to include enough information in A and B so the reader is motivated to take step C. Make sure the reader clearly understands what you're selling and what's good about it, including comparisons or proof of your product's advantages. In this case, of course, your product is real estate and discount properties. Try to avoid lengthy case studies or anecdotes.

If you're offering a service, explain it in terms of the real benefits people get from using it. Instead of "Helping Those Facing Foreclosure" say, "We offer workable plans to avoid foreclosure."

Use People Talk

Write your ad in a conversational tone, as if you're talking directly to the individual reading it. Avoid passive language such as "our services are designed for…" Instead, use active language such as "we've designed our services for..." The weak verb "are" has been changed to an active verb, "designed." Also, don't forget that while you're trying to communicate in a conversational tone, what you're saying is still in print. Always make sure your ads are grammatically correct.

Offer Something Free

In most cases, your ad is only the fuse that ignites a productive business relationship. Often, the next step in the relationship is where the customer asks for and receives more details about your company or what you're offering. Use wisdom in how you can make that next step as attractive to them as possible.

Which of the following is more appealing? "Reply now for more information," or "Reply now for our free special report, *Six Steps To Financing your New Home*."

Make It Easy To Respond

Offer your readers as many ways to respond as possible. Include your phone number or other contact information in your reply statement. Never miss a chance to publish your websites and blog site URLs. Don't cut yourself off from potential business by failing to offer communication options.

Check Your Ad's Position Regularly

Online classified ad areas change quickly. The ad you posted yesterday to the first screen of ad titles will today be pushed down two or three screens by the influx of ads posted after yours. Ads located on the first two or three screens are far more likely to be read than ones buried further down.

Check the ad's position each day to make sure your ad hasn't slipped down into oblivion. If it has, re-post the ad with a similar title to move it back up in the list again.

Use Multiple Postings and Coded Responses

Your ad may fit into more than one classification on an online service, or you may be able to tailor it so that it does. A customized ad for each area will magnify your visibility. On the other hand, don't post the same ad to several different areas just for the sake of visibility—such "cross-posting" will identify you as someone too lazy to make sure their ads are appropriate for each area. Never mind that such ads could be rejected by the ad area or newsgroup's moderator, such ads could cause the people you're trying to reach to ignore all of your posts entirely.

When you post a series of tailored ads in different places, use different response keywords so you'll be able to tell which ad or ads are pulling the best. That way, you'll know which ads are doing better by the words people use in their replies.

Free Special Report
How to Repair your Credit and Purchase your Dream Home for only 1% Down Pymt

Summary

Classified ads are popular because they work. But like any marketing weapon, they work only if you know how to make the most of them. Follow these strategies when creating and placing your ads, and you'll be well ahead of the competition.

The Magic and Tragic Words of Marketing

Magic words propel great ideas towards profitability. Tragic words doom great ideas to failure. Successful marketers know the difference. A lot of people realize that a great idea must be expressed with great words. But only successful marketers actually *know* those words.

If you're creating a marketing strategy, you ought to start becoming aware of these words, and enrich your marketing vocabulary (not to mention your bank account) by using them liberally. I have this suspicion that magic words in your marketing materials lead to magic numbers in your financial statements.

Successful marketing is concerned not only with *what* you say in your marketing, but also with *how* you say it. Saying the right thing with the wrong words is a waste of time and money, in addition to being a preventable error. Ouch!

One of the more intriguing aspects of the magic words is their durability. Hard-nosed marketers have been using many of these words since the turn of the *last* century, with these words still generating sales for successful marketers all across the nation.

Most of these words have been verified in daily usage since Day One of marketing, yet they maintain their magic. "I love you" will never sound trite. Certain words have the power to turn prospects on and motivate them to think the right thoughts about your business. Other words have the power to turn prospects off and cause them to think thoughts that could be detrimental to your business. Can you write potent marketing copy without magic words? Yes. It's also possible to walk from San Francisco to New York on your knees.

Here are words successful marketers are using to win profits and influence people:

FREE	LOVE	SAFE	WANTED
BENEFITS	RIGHT	YOU	ALTERNATIVE
SECURITY	SALE	NOW	WINNINGS
ONLINE	VALUE	FUN	PROVEN
GAINE	MONEY	HAPPY	DISCOVER
HOW TO	ADVICE	NEW	INTRODUCING
PRECIOUS	YOUR	SAVE	SUDDENLY
PROUD	PEOPLE	SECRET	GUARANTEED
NATURAL	FAST	EASY	HEALTHY
SOLUTION	MAGIC	WHY	COMFORTABLE

These words carry a great deal of weight. Use them in your advertising, brochures, signs, E-mails, websites, blogs, telemarketing, presentations—wherever you can. They describe what people want.

They make people read on. They offer things that people are looking for.

As there are magic words to speed you on to marketing success, there are *tragic* words that lead somewhere you don't want your readers to go. Many marketers know the pain of marketing that didn't pull. But few of them know that one tiny word may have been the reason. So as not to be guilty of word abuse, stay on the alert for these tragic words in any of your marketing:

BUY	DIFFICULT	DEATH	OBLIGATION
WRONG	FAILURE	ORDER	DECISION
FAIL	BAD	DEAL	COST
SELL	LIABILITY	WORRY	LOSS
HARD	DETAILS	LOSE	CONTRACT

These words make readers lose interest and stop reading. They can undermine your marketing effort. Undoubtedly, there are uglier words than these in the language as well as more beautiful words than the magic words. But in marketing, beautiful refers only to the looks of your financial statement. The marketing battlefields are littered with dead marketing campaigns that were undermined by words that were trendy or faddish. It is very uncool to use such words.

Successful marketers stick with the magic and avoid the tragic.

Chapter 4:
Video Marketing

Marketing Resource #13: Use www.YouTube.com for uploading the videos that you have created; this one site gets over two billion views a day. (See the following chapter for directions on how to create your own videos.)

Marketing Resource #14: Use www.TrafficGeyserStore.com to distribute videos to many locations.

Marketing Resource #15: www.MetaCafe.com is a site where you can upload videos; however, it is geared more toward professionals. MetaCafe looks for broadly entertaining videos, not uniquely personal ones.

Marketing Resource #16: www.DailyMotion.com is a video sharing service website that is based in Paris, France. It began business about the same time as YouTube.

Marketing Resource #17: www.UStream.tv is yet another site that offers the ability to create and post your own videos. UStream also offers the capability of posting streaming video on your site.

Marketing Resource #18: www.Viddler.com is an interactive online video platform for uploading, sharing, enhancing, tagging, commenting on, and forming groups around videos. Viddler provides a free service for non-commercial users, but there is also a paid business service.

Marketing Resource #19: www.TubeMogul.com is an online video distribution company. When you upload a video to TubeMogul, their system automatically submits it to several online video websites. This saves time and generates exposure. Some of the sites include YouTube, Yahoo, MySpace, MetaCafe, Google, DailyMotion, and more. This is a free service!

Video Marketing Made Easy

It's no secret that the Internet has changed everything about the way people do business today. I talk to many real estate investors who tend to shy away from all that technology and the Internet offers to them. There are many reasons why they do this. For some, it's overwhelming and they aren't sure where to begin. Others feel inadequate and believe it's just too difficult.

Much of why I have written this book is to 1) break marketing down into bite-sized, manageable pieces that anyone can take on, and 2) simplify different methods and show you just how easy and simple it can be.

This is particularly true in the area of video marketing. At first glance, video marketing seems a formidable and daunting task. But after reading this chapter, you'll see just how easy it really is and you'll kick yourself for having waited so long to add it to your marketing regime.

Advantages of Videos

Let's look at some of the advantages of using videos. First of all, this is an excellent way to connect with your prospects. Your personality and your message can be shown on the Net twenty-four hours a day, seven days a week. Your site visitors (or blog visitors, etc.) who are browsing the Net at two in the morning will have access to your personalized information. Those who watch the video are getting acquainted with you simply by "tuning in."

There are many free services to place your videos. This is a big plus. See the Marketing Resources at the beginning of this chapter.

If you think you have to be a professional videographer, think again.

It is okay to have an amateurish looking video as it gives the video more character. Very little editing, if any, is needed.

You can shoot the video directly from your computer camera on your computer or you can purchase an iFlip. You shoot the message, plug in and upload and Viola! You have a show online.

There are of course, many ways to drive traffic to your site, but using videos is one of the easiest and one of the fastest growing advertising segments online.

YouTube

The biggest online video service is one you've no doubt heard of, and that is www.YouTube.com. If you are not at present utilizing this incredible resource, I encourage you to get on over to the site, set up your account and begin uploading videos to it frequently.

YouTube is the second largest search engine in the world right behind its parent company, Google. I have seen statistics that claim there are over a billion videos watched per month on YouTube (Bits.Blogs.NYTimes.com/2010/06/01/youtube-dominates-online-video-views). This equals a TON of possible traffic to your real estate investing website.

Getting Started

I want to show you different ways to create videos and to maximize the time it takes to do this activity. I will also share some basic scripts to get you going and to help you launch out into some successful video marketing.

The first thing you must figure out is who you want to attract into your marketing *funnel* with this video.

Is it:

- Real estate buyers on the retail side?
- Motivated real estate sellers?
- Real estate investors who want to buy discount properties?

Remember that it is crucial to ask this before doing *any* type of marketing. This is what is known as target marketing. Once you catch on to how easy this is, it's a piece of cake.

Once you have selected your target market (or your audience) there are many different approaches to each one of those prospects. Let's look at the example of targeting to real estate buyers.

We can sell the house on a *Rent to Own* agreement. If so, you would then want to educate your prospect on what they need to do to qualify for a rent-to-own deal. This instruction could be broken up into multiple videos. I would try to keep each video under five minutes since most people who browse the Internet have a short attention span, and little patience. They want to grab the information and move on.

How To Begin

You might begin with Video 1, which would be the welcome video and would simply explain the whole concept of rent-to-own plans and how they can be set up. At the close you will tell them to watch Video #2. Be sure to tell your visitor to go to your site and opt in for more videos. For instance you might say, "If you like this video get on over to [insert your Squeeze Page URL here] where you'll find even more high-quality teaching videos."

Believe me when I say that people enjoy these kinds of training videos. They are getting to know you, they are learning new information, and they feel you have now given them a gift of considerable value.

Let's look at another example. Say you have a property for sale.

Drive up to this property with a little iFlip in hand. You can say something like:

"Hello my name is _________________. I'm with www.YourURL.com. I'm at 123 Any Town Street right now. As you can see, it's a very nice 3-bedroom, 2-bath home sitting on a cul-de-sac with a fenced in back yard with great trees. As you can also see, the houses in the surrounding neighborhood are also exceptionally nice houses.

"Now we're approaching the front door. Take a look at this attractive entrance to the home. We are now walking into the front hallway. Notice the hard wood floors, the spacious 8-foot ceilings. Would you look at this new paint in the living room."

As you continue with the tour, always add a "call to action" at the close. Encourage that viewer to go to your website to get the rest of the details. Remember you are always creating ways to streamline your "leads funnel," and this is one of those ways.

This is super simple and easy to do. You don't even need to be on camera with this method. You are just walking through the house with a camera in hand, leading your viewers on the grand tour, so to speak. Talk as though you are chatting with a friend. Let your personality come through. Have fun with it.

I hope your imagination is working ahead of me and that you've already realized that this same technique will work with all properties from rental properties, to commercial buildings or single family homes, the ugly and the nice alike. So utilize this simple tool and leverage it to the fullest.

Now that the video is tagged, the next step is to make sure your Squeeze Page address is on the video. This is simple and easy and can be done with basic video editing software. You can get such software online. To locate it just go to Google.com and type in "Free Video Editing Software."

Browse through the selections shown and find the one that fits your criteria and go from there.

Channel Viewers to the Website

You have a chance to be seen by thousands of people around the world through your video. The main purpose of your video then is to channel these viewers to your website. While there, they will put their name and E-mail into your system. This allows you to market to them and begin building a long-term relationship.

Here's an outline of a basic script:

Intro: *Hello! Mark Evans DM here with MarkEvansDM.com*

Body: Put your content here. When creating your video always mention your URL (address) at least twice—once at the beginning and again at the end.

Exit: Well, I hope this video helps you get moving in the right direction. To get more great videos and free information visit my website at www.MarkEvansDM.com. I'll see you there!

You see now just how easy it is to add this vital bit of information. Some will hear your website address and some will see it. Some will see *and* hear it. This may be the only impetus needed to drive them to your webpage.

I hope you are starting to see the power in this simple strategy of using videos to start marketing your real estate business.

There are many different sites that you can upload your videos to—and the more the merrier. Below I'll give you a few ideas in how to get this moving today!

Video Distribution

If you are like me and you don't like uploading to every single video service out there, then check this out. There is a great service that allows you to upload your video one time and then let their system distribute to the sites that you select. This is a huge time saver. Depending where you are in your business, you will definitely want to take a closer look at this service. This is the same service I use: www.TrafficGeyserStore.com.

So here's your action plan:

Step 1: Go to www.YouTube.com and set up your account for your videos. This might take all of five minutes or less. Consider using your website address or your business name as your YouTube username. This presents a more professional appearance.

Step 2: Ask yourself this question: Who do you want to attract to your marketing funnel? Grab a blank sheet of paper and begin to brainstorm of all the ideas you have on what to shoot a video about.

Step 3: Now that you have selected your target market audience, you will want to create a simple script on what to say. Be sure to set a time limit on this. If you don't, you'll never get it out of the gate. I'd say 30 minutes or less will do just fine.

Step 4: Will it be perfect? Absolutely not. You will probably mess up, but that's okay. Just get the video up and get it onto YouTube.com as quickly as possible. You can always delete it once you get your next one out there. Like anything else in life, you will get better and better with practice.

Sample Script

Below I've given you a simple script to use to get your first video done:

Hello, I'm ____________________with www.YourURL.com. I'm excited to be sharing this video with you. You're in for a real treat. Over the next few weeks and months, you will be learning a great deal of amazing information here, so make sure you check back often to learn more about ______________ (How to make money in real estate, How to buy a house, How to sell a house). We are here to help you any way we can. In the meantime be sure to visit me at www.YourURL.com to get more free information.

Set a Deadline and Do It!

The key factor in accomplishing any of the marketing techniques offered in this book is to set a deadline for yourself. This is important in jumpstarting the activity. I challenge you to stop reading right now and do steps one through four and clear away the confusion. Do it as soon as possible.

You've already seen how easy it is to do this. Trust me, you can set up your account, set up your video and then have it broadcasting out to the world within 32-minutes from start to finish.

If you are doing this for the first time, your first one will be the most difficult (if you can even call it difficult). After that, everything's a piece of cake.

So put this book down, get going, and time yourself.

Summary

As you can see from above it's all about doing it, not just reading about it and thinking on it. Let's be honest—we all procrastinate, but the people who jump in and do it are the ones who will win big over time.

Once you have your own Squeeze Pages (see Chapter 5), and perhaps your own blog (see Chapter 6), you can also upload your videos on these highly personalized sites. Social networking is yet another tool you can utilize when you want to upload videos—such as your profile pages on FaceBook and LinkedIn (see Chapter 7).

Chapter 5:
Your Real Estate Investing Squeeze Pages

Marketing Resource #20: Build your own personalized Squeeze Pages (or have them built) and see to it that it is filled with interactive features that say "come on in" to the site visitor.
www.VirtualRealEstateWebsites.com

Your Squeeze Page is the Heart and Soul of Online Marketing

Personally, it's difficult for me to imagine real estate investors in this day and time trying to run their businesses without Squeeze Pages. I know it is done, but as I said, it's difficult for me to imagine being efficient. And I say why make it any harder to do business then we have to.

Personalized Squeeze Pages are the heart and soul of your online marketing thrust. Almost everything else you do both online and offline can work in tandem by driving prospects to your Squeeze Page where you will capture contact information and build your contact lists.

As with other aspects of technology, I find that some real estate investors are intimidated by the thought of creating their own personalized Squeeze Pages. By letting this intimidation have the last say, these investors are missing out on one of the most powerful marketing tools available today.

Build-Your-Own Squeeze Page

Years ago, creating your own Squeeze Page (or paying to have one created) was a huge—and expensive—undertaking. But no more. The www.VirtualRealEstateWebsites.com service offers customizable Squeeze Page solutions for real estate investors. (See more about these services in Chapter 11.)

We'll be talking more about outsourcing in Chapter 10; however, suffice to say that you can easily outsource this project if even the easiest site builder is not your cup of tea. Plan on investing around $1,000 - $5,000 plus a monthly hosting fee. I prefer you not waste your time and energy, because today, you can quickly set up sites with all the bells and whistles that are used by investors all over the world. And you can do this for the cost of less than a cup of coffee a day. They are good and you can set them up in 10 minutes or less. Heck, they can even make you money without you ever doing a real estate deal which is great for you. I love what technology can do for you in this business.

Alive and Interactive

The key to an effective Squeeze Page in today's market is that the site be alive and interactive. From reading the chapter on videos, you already know how very simple it is to create a video. You can upload your videos onto your personalized Squeeze Pages. Let your personality shine through with photos of you, your business, and perhaps even your family. Become a real person to the site visitor.

This is also a great place to include testimonies from your satisfied clients. If you have no testimonies, it can only be one of two reasons: 1) You have as yet not completed any deals, or 2) You're not asking for positive feedback. Every time you close a deal, be sure to ask for testimonies. Nothing speaks louder than a happy, satisfied client. Don't waste this important resource.

Add Resources

Add links on your Squeeze Page to other resources that homebuyers, investors, or sellers may be interested in. This again shows your concern and involvement in their success. A link to your personal blog is also a great idea. (See more about blogs in Chapter 6.)

Here is where you will offer those free reports and, in doing so, you will capture contact information and begin to build a quality list (see Chapter 9).

Summary

Think of your Squeeze Page as your storefront. Here you are at your best 24/7! A good website never sleeps, never takes a lunch break, and never even takes a smoke break. This is the place were relationships are created and built.

Now do you see why I can't imagine an investor doing business in today's market without a website? It would be like a farmer still using a yoke of oxen to plow his fields. It may get the job done, but at what cost?

Marketing Yourself

Once you understand that people judge you from the first moment you meet them (whether in person or online), and realize that there is a range of tools available to help support your positioning, you can be more successful in every encounter.

Positioning Yourself

If you haven't already guessed, a key part of marketing yourself is learning how to position yourself. The people you meet just aren't going to take the time to really get to know you. They're going to make a snap decision about who you are and what you stand for whether you want them to or not.

Most of us don't like to accept this. Most of us don't want to boil the essence of our personality down to just eight words. Most of us don't have a plan and a solid goal. And most of us fail more than we ought to.

Eight Words

Abraham Lincoln has a *position* in our brains. *Honest guy with beard who freed the slaves.* Eight words. Compare this with Grover Cleveland, Millard Fillmore, U.S. Grant and even Lyndon Johnson. These Presidents all worked hard, but because they have no position, they're anonymous.

Not convinced? Think positioning only works for famous people? Think about your high school days. Who do you remember? Why? Chances are the people who stand out in your memory aren't necessarily the ones you spent the most time with, but they are the ones with the most vivid positioning. Did they do this consciously? Probably not. Doesn't matter. Unconscious or not, positioning effects the way you're perceived.

We know ourselves very, very well. We're aware of all of our skills, our talents, our strengths and our weaknesses. And quite often, we expect that others will too. We meet someone at a party and are surprised and offended when they walk off after just a couple of minutes. "Wait! I'm so interesting! How can you leave?"

Unfortunately, most people aren't as interested in you as you are. If you want people to remember something about you, you need to choose a position.

You Choose

Of course, no one can force you to market yourself. You can reject the entire system and insist on *being yourself*. That's your privilege.

If you don't consciously choose a position, you still have one. It may be muddy, inconsistent and difficult to detect, but just about everyone you meet is going to pick one for you anyway. You may think, "I don't want to do any marketing for myself." But that just means that the marketing you are doing, consciously or unconsciously, probably won't help you achieve your goals.

This is one of the key messages of marketing. You must choose a position or have it chosen for you.

Be Consistent

Successful marketers learn early on that they must select their own position, that they must consistently use it and they have to stick with it. The position you choose for yourself will determine who you become friends with, where you work and how high you get promoted. Of course your position will evolve. It can grow and change with you.

Capture Your Essence

The message behind positioning yourself isn't to invent something brand new out of whole cloth. In fact, it's exactly the opposite. You position yourself well when you capture part of your essence in a few simple symbols and phrases. You must choose a position you can live with, a position you can be proud of, a position you can deliver on.

All too often, people unconsciously position themselves in very unattractive ways. These are good people, talented people, but people who are sabotaging their lives by focusing on an element of their personality that others dislike.

The way you look, the way you talk, the way you act, the way you offer your online presence, all work to support or tear down the image (your positioning) you establish for yourself.

Take the time to sum up your position in eight short words. Work on it until you're happy with it. And then let it evolve.

Nearly every marketing Resource in this book lends itself to establishing and furthering your position. Use them to your positioning advantage.

Chapter 6:
Writing Your Way to Success

In this chapter we will review a number of ways in which writing plays a big part in your marketing strategies. There are many areas online in which writing will exponentially expand your online presence. And, as I mentioned earlier, each one of these can be outsourced. Let's begin with writing articles.

Articles

Marketing Resource #21: www.EzineArticles.com is the premier of all article submission sites. This is the best place to begin building your articles library as it lends a strong sense of credibility to you and your business.

Marketing Resource #22: www.GoArticles.com comes next in popularity. This is also a viable site that has earned respect online for their caliber of materials.

Marketing Resource #23: www.ArticleDashboard.com is pretty much on par with GoArticles. Again, always read the submission guides for each site and comply with them.

Use Your Knowledge to Write Articles

Because you have the Internet at your fingertips, you can become a researcher to share information. Take those bits of information and turn them into 300- to 500-word articles and get them out into cyberspace. If that sounds boring and dead-end, let me give you clearer insight.

There are numerous sites on the Net where articles are published and distributed. Each article goes out with a *resource box* intact. That resource box is created by the author of the article. It can contain your personal and business bio, business information, and links to your blog and/or Squeeze Pages.

People browsing the web go to these articles sites for information the same way they might run a Google search. Additionally, people who publish Ezines (online magazines) are always looking for great articles. When they find one (through an article site) that they like, they download it (resource box and all) and publish it in their Ezine. This is called "viral" growth, because your resource information is growing throughout the Internet like a virus—only in a good way.

The premier article site is www.EzineArticles.com. They have very strict guidelines stating that all articles are to be informational only—no selling or promoting. No links are to be in the body of the article, but in the resource box only. Other sites such as GoArticles and ArticleDashboard allow links within the body of the article. Be sure to read the guidelines and follow them to the letter!

Avoid Submission Tools

You will find ads that offer tools to help you submit articles to all of the many articles sites. After all, if a few articles are great, hundreds of submissions would be even better, right? Wrong. Resist the temptation since the Google *spiders* are finely tuned to spot spam, no matter how legitimate the article may look on the surface.

Keep your integrity intact by setting up a regimen of writing an article or two a month and submitting them to three or four article sites. In a year or so, you'll have a great library to your credit. Be sure you include all pertinent information in the resources box.

Again, if this sounds like nothing you want to do, then outsource the job (See Chapter 10). But don't neglect this incredibly effective marketing tool.

Blogs

Marketing Resource #24: www.Blogger.com is by far the easiest blog site to use. This is a Google product and interacts well if you maintain a Google E-mail. No fees here. This is totally free advertising and marketing.

Marketing Resource #25: www.WordPress.com has a free version and also a fee-based upgrade. The upgrade, of course, offers more bells and whistles. The one you choose depends on your needs and your technological savvy.

A Blog is an Online Journal

Yet another area in which writing plays a big part is blogs. If you are unfamiliar with what a blog actually is, it's rather like an online journal. The term is short for "web log." In the early days of the Internet, blogs were mostly chitchat between friends and relatives. However, in today's business world, many major business entities maintain blogs to establish themselves as experts in their fields.

If you have taken my advice about writing articles on a regular basis, I have good news for you. Those articles can be turned into blog entries. And blog entries can become articles. This is one of the ways in which you can work smart, not hard.

If you will post content to your blog on a regular basis and give needed information related to your field (real estate) people who are interested in the topic will want to visit your site and you will create a following.

Setting Up Your Blog

As I stressed with creating Squeeze Pages, setting up a blog site is very *very* simple to do. Two of the most popular blogs sites are www.Blogger.com and www.WordPress.com. If you can follow directions at all, you can easily set up your own blog. There are many attractive and professional templates to choose from. You'll be amazed at how your professional your page will look.

When you first begin, you will be asked to create your user profile. Here's yet another opportunity to let the world know who you are, an opportunity to create a status as an expert in your field.

Provide Useful Information

Give your readers information and insight into how to find the right house, or tips to sell a house, or creative ways to find financing. By offering visitors what they want, they will come back for more. Be sure to add your website link at the bottom of every blog post.

Your personal blog site is an area you will not want to neglect. Nothing can be more detrimental to your integrity as a neglected blog site. If you see that you simply cannot carve out the time to keep it updated, this is an area you will want to think about outsourcing (see Chapter 10).

Action Step

Create your own personalized blog wherein you can expand your online presence by offering quality information and needed resources. You can upload videos, create links, and funnel visitors to your Squeeze Page.

AutoResponder Letters

Marketing Resource #26: One of the premier autoresponder sites is www.DiscountEmailFollowup.com. It's easy to use and offers great customer support and great tutorials.

Marketing Resource #27: The prices and features at www.GetReponse.com are similar to those offered above. Which one is best usually comes down to personal preference. Either way, you can't lose.

Autoresponders: Set It and Forget It

If you have started writing articles and creating blog entries, with a little bit of editing these can become autoresponder letters to your prospects. An autoresponder is by far one of the best marketing tools you have access to.

If you are unfamiliar with autoresponders, it is a way to have E-mails sent to your prospects on a regular basis. It's a "set it and forget it" system.

While you may have never used an autoresponder yourself, you have received hundreds of them into your E-mail box. Remember when you signed up for that newsletter? Or signed up for a series of tutorial E-mails? The reason those arrived in your E-mail box with such regularity is because the sender used an autoresponder.

The idea is to write a series of letters, enter them into your autoresponder account site, set them to go out at various intervals and then sit back and let them work. Obviously, each one will contain your Squeeze Pages and blog URLs.

Above I have listed two of the best autoresponder sites. Each one contains easy-to-follow, step-by-step tutorials. The list you are mailing to is made up of the contacts you have captured from your Squeeze Pages. This growing list will soon become invaluable to you.

In addition to what we call "drip" marketing (slowly dripping E-mails to the recipient), you can also send one blanket E-mail to all of your contacts. Say you just came upon a great investment property and you want all the rehabbers on your list to know about it. It's a simple thing to let them know via an autoresponder E-mail. Create one message and send to all—talk about time saving and easy to do!

This is not a free service, but the monthly fees are extremely reasonable in light of the service it renders and for the return you get back. This is truly a must-have to stay sane and make it big in the real estate business.

Newsletters

Marketing Resource #28: www.DiscountEmailFollowup.com offers E-mail marketing resources that also includes newsletters. They also offer newsletter tutorial. It's a low-cost monthly service fee that is well worth it.

Keep In Touch

One of the best ways to keep in touch with prospects (or clients, either one) is with a weekly, monthly or quarterly newsletter. Personally, I prefer weekly. This is a non-threatening way to keep up ongoing communication and let people know what you're up to. Your newsletter can be sent online or by snail mail. You may want to make this a part of your offline marketing strategy (See Chapter 8). A physical newsletter that your recipient can hold and refer back to can make a powerful impression, but there is, of course, a cost to printing and mailing a physical newsletter.

Your newsletter can contain newsy items about your business, and also feature properties that you have available at the time.

eBooks

Marketing Resource #22: Use your existing writings—articles or blog entries—and compile them to create an eBook. Use www.Elance.com or www.Guru.com to outsource this work (see Chapter 10). Your eBook can be given as a freebie, or sold for a reasonable price to create an additional stream of income. Place these offers on your own website (see Chapter 5).

Marketing Resource #23: If you have never before created a PDF file check out www.PDF995.com. This is a free software download that makes creating PDF files so simple a fifth grader could do it! (You'll soon find a million uses for it beyond making your eBook.)

A Product of Value

Have you ever thought about writing a book? If you can write an article, if you can write a special report, you can write an eBook. (See Chapter 6 for more tips on writing.) Your eBook provides a great service to your site visitors—especially if you give it away for free. Even if you charge a reasonable price, you are still providing a product of value that helps your prospects.

Put as much of your individual personality into the book as possible. When you do your eBook, it will help your audience to know you better, and will serve to build relationships.

Once you have written ten articles, now you actually have ten chapters for an eBook. As you look at your articles, is there one main theme running through them? Can you see a way to pull them together in a cohesive fashion?

Throughout the book, you will be careful to weave in links to your websites and your blog. As with articles, you will create a viral growth of your contact information.

If you have the basic foundations for a book (or even just the idea for one) and have no time to complete it yourself, this is another project that you may want to outsource (see Chapter 10).

Once the eBook is completed, put it into a PDF file, upload it to your website and blog and get it out there for the world to see.

Press Releases

Marketing Resource #30: www.1888pressrelease.com offers services that include free press release submission, press release distribution, sample press releases, press release writing tips, and the most popular press releases. These services are free.

Marketing Resource #31: www.PRLog.org is another viable free press release service. All of their services are free.

Marketing Resource #32: www.PRBuzz.com requires a per-year fee, but is highly effective.

Expand Your Exposure With Press Releases

A press release is another area that requires good writing. It is a resource that is highly overlooked by real estate investors. Most people relate press releases to a publicity agent who creates a professional publicity kit in which press releases would be included. If this is your mindset, think again. A press release is nothing more than a notice letting people know of an event that is happening in your business.

In the past, press releases were sent out by mail to scores of media destinations, such as newspapers, and TV and radio stations. Nowadays, there is a wide variety of websites that deal exclusively in handling press releases, and many are free. The great thing about these sites is that they offer tutorials on the correct way to write and layout a press release. That means if you know nothing about how to write a press release, you can quickly learn.

As with articles, you will find many services that offer to send your releases to scores of other press release sites.

Make it Newsworthy

The process of creating a press release is simple. First of all, make sure your release is talking about something that is actually newsworthy. For instance, you have partnered with other businesses to sponsor a charity event. Never use a press release as a place to advertise your business or your services. That's not the goal. The goal is exposure, to get your name and the name of your business before the public eye.

While it is not meant to be an ad, every press release will go out bearing your name, the name of your business, your location, and your website addresses. Every release will work to drive readers to your websites.

Distribution

Once your release is written (never make them longer than one page) choose one or two free press release distribution sites. (See those listed at the beginning of this section.)

Select sites that will add your release to the news engines. There are big distribution sites who charge a hefty fee, but the good news is that free sites work just as well.

After your release has been distributed online, be sure and post it on your blog. In fact, you might want to create a Press Release Archives, so visitors can see what you've been up to in the past.

Local News Releases

If your release is about something of local interest, as in the example of sponsoring a charity event, send it to your local newspaper. Or perhaps your community has a "neighborhood" newspaper that is always on the lookout for newsworthy items (most are). Become friends with the staff there and let them know what you're all about. They will soon be looking for items of interest coming from you and your business.

You won't be churning out press releases in the same way that you will with articles. However, if you think outside the box and get creative, you'll find a wide variety of reasons to create a press release. And when you do, you are once again increasing exposure! And every time you increase exposure, you discover new ways to capture leads.

Summary

As you can see, using your writing skills will open a number of doors to creating expansive exposure for your business. Every one of these writing opportunities will work to drive traffic to your websites and to create more leads than you ever dreamed you could have. And you will see the results in a growing profit margin in your business.

You Are What You Write

Writing ability is the single most important weapon you can wield in cyberspace. The words you write are your best and often only chance to create an impression on customers. Just as your confidence in an off-line vendor is affected by that person's command of the language, your prospects' opinion of you in cyberspace is affected by your command of the written word. Before you will ever have the chance to impress customers with your superior service, expertise, or follow-up, many of your prospects will decide whether or not to do business with you by the quality of your written communications.

None of us likes to think our writing skills need improving, and even fewer of us are willing to spend the time and energy to improve them. But consider this: your larger and better-financed competitors pay professional writers to create their storefront copy, produce electronic publications and brochures, and perhaps even pen their e-mail for them. In order to compete, you must develop the same professionalism in your writing.

Professionalism in writing means:

Correctness

Messages filled with errors tell everyone that you don't care enough about your online presence to get it right. Strive to eliminate spelling, grammar, or formatting errors from all you online messages. If you can't spot the errors, have someone else proofread your text or pick up a good business-writing guide at your local bookstore.

Clarity

Use words that say exactly what you mean to say. Vague or ambiguous messages cause confusion that will either abort a budding business relationship entirely, or force you to waste time sending further messages before making your point.

Economy

Say what you have to say in as little space as possible. Nobody in cyberspace has enough time, so any message that wastes time automatically gets a negative reception. Respect your prospect and customer's time by keeping messages brief and to the point.

Personality

Infuse as much of your business identity into a message as possible, and speak directly to the individual reader. Use the same words and figures of speech you use in day-to-day conversation, and envision a specific person as your correspondent whenever you write something. The pros also know that using words like you, we, us, and our, makes a message much more personal. Everyone who reads your message should feel as if the message is directed specifically to him or her.

So rather than dashing off messages without a second thought, give your writing the same care and consideration you would use in designing a print ad or reviewing the copy for a printed brochure.

It means an extra investment of time, but the payoff will be a better online presence, higher customer confidence, and a fatter bottom line.

Chapter 7:
Marketing Online

You may be looking at this chapter title and thinking, "But we already discussed online advertising, because most of the resources mentioned for classified ads are online."

While that is true, classified ads comprise only a tip of the iceberg when it comes to online advertising. In this chapter we will look at a number of other means for marketing online using the power of the Internet to grow your business. This is known as PPC marketing or "Pay Per Click" marketing.

Pay-Per-Click Marketing

Marketing Resource #33: Go to www.AdWords.Google.com to learn the details about how to incorporate this technique into your ongoing marketing strategy.
Marketing Resource #34: www.SearchMarketing.Yahoo.com is the Yahoo! version of Pay Per Click.
Marketing Resource #35: www.AdCenter.Microsoft.com will take you to the advertising center for Microsoft.

Pay Per Click

Entire books have been written about AdWords and how they work. AdWords is the name of the Google Pay Per Click program. If you pull up any Google search page, the AdWords advertisements appear in the top two positions above the *natural* listings and also in the boxes on the right of the page. For instance, if you searched the term "real estate investing," you would see ads appear on the page that someone wrote and then submitted via their AdWords account.

Quite simply this is how it works: Your ads appear beside related search results; people see the ad and click on it, and then connect to your business. Rather than paying for an ad as in conventional advertising, you only pay when someone actually clicks on your ad to get more information (hence the term "pay per click").

Keywords are the backbone of this type of advertising. Within your AdWords account you are able to enter keywords to use to determine ad placement. A keyword bid is the amount of money that you, as the advertiser, are willing to spend per click to get a prospect to your site.

It's easy to budget exactly how much you want to spend per day on your venture and therefore you are totally in control at all times. It's important to note that all search engines offer some type of similar pay-per-click advertising.

Setting up an AdWords account (or its equivalent) may be something you want to explore as your business continues to grow.

eBay

Marketing Resource #36: Learn more about real estate listing on eBay at www.eBay.com/RealEstate

I'm always surprised to learn how few of my fellow real estate investors are aware of eBay's real estate section. Most see eBay as a place where items are auctioned. However, while you can auction, that is not the only option for real estate on eBay. It's possible to list your property in their real estate pages for 30 days for a *set insertion fee.*

When you think of the incredible exposure of such a site as eBay, you might want to consider this avenue for drawing contacts to your website!

Online Auctions

Marketing Resource #37: www.Bid4Assets.com provides a venue where you can auction your properties or pick up a few choice bargains. Either way, this site will provide it and the services are free.

If an auction is in your game plan, there are sites that provide such venues. Of course you can use the auction aspect of eBay, or you can try Bid4Assets.

Yahoo!

Marketing Resource #38: Check out the Yahoo! real estate details at www.Yahoo.com/RealEstate

The familiar search engine known as Yahoo! boasts a vibrant advertising section, not the least of which is their real estate section. You will post your ad nationwide and reach the Internet's largest classified audience. Your ad runs for 21 days and is viewable when users search classifieds on Yahoo! Real Estate. There is a listing fee for this service.

Facebook

Marketing Resource #39: Visit www.Facebook.com/Advertising to learn all of the ins and outs regarding advertising on Facebook.

Facebook, like eBay and Yahoo!, is a much overlooked resource for advertising. In fact, few people even know that you *can* advertise on the highly popular social networking site.

With Facebook, you can target your audience geographically and also by demographics such as age range. It works like AdWords in that you pay per click rather than by the ad itself. With a current count of global participants of over 400 million, you can easily see why FaceBook is an incredible way to gain exposure.

Banner Ads

Marketing Resource #40: Go to www.AdDesigner.com to learn more about how to design your own banner ads. Use the high-quality banner ads you design through AdDesigner to get higher click-through rates (which means more traffic to your website), to build a professional image for your website, and to create a favorable impression with those who see your professional banner ads.

Marketing Resource #41: www.MyBannerMaker.com is another free service for creating your own banner ads. However, their own "branding bar" will show up on the banners that are free. They offer fee-based VIP services where the branding bar is removed.

Marketing Resource #42: www.20DollarBanners.com is a great user-friendly site to get banners made at an affordable price. Tell them your thoughts and they create from there.

Banners Still Work

You'll hear a lot of pros and cons about online banner ads. Some say they are a nuisance and that, while they were once a real novelty, nowadays no one pays them any mind. The truth is that savvy business people still use them, and site visitors still click on them. Many are colorful and full of lively graphics to grabs the visitor's attention and compels him or her to click for more information.

The great thing about banner ads is that banner ad space can be purchased on a website or blog that is complementary to, but not in competition with, your business. That banner can be linked to your Squeeze Pages, and will be an effective tool to drive traffic to your site. For instance, you may want to contact local mortgage brokers about placing a banner on their websites or blogs. With a little imagination, you can come up with a wide variety of places where your ad would be beneficial.

The neat thing about banner ads is that you can design your own. Make it look like you want it to look, and say what you want it to say. If you have a unique logo, that can be placed on the banner as well. If this is a marketing strategy that you have previously ignored, it may be time to give it a closer look.

Real-Estate-Specific Websites

Marketing Resource #43: www.PropFrog.com* This is by far the best investor's secret weapon to growing your buyers list and to selling deals fast. You can set up a free account and blast your properties to be seen by millions of eyeballs. Hop over there now and set up your free account to start building your business. (Did I mention that this is free?)

I would literally put this book down right now and set up your free account.

Marketing Resource #44: www.Rent-To-Own-Ads.com charges a fee of $10 per six-month listing.

Marketing Resource #45: Fees at www.ForSaleByOwner.com start at $80 a month. This is a vastly popular site with a great deal of traffic.

Marketing Resource #46: www.IRentToOwn.com*

Marketing Resource #47: www.DomesticSale.com/RealEstate*

Marketing Resource #48: www.FrontDoor.com*

Marketing Resource #49: www.Trulia.com*

Marketing Resource #50: www.Enormo.com is a global site for real estate agents to list properties.

Marketing Resource #51:www.ByOwnerMLS.com*

Marketing Resource #52: www.HomeSaleWizard.com*

Marketing Resource #53: www.MyNextRehab.com is targeted more toward investors than toward buyers or sellers.

Marketing Resource #54: www.Zillow.com is used by many investors to find the value of a property; however, don't forget this is a great site to list your properties. You'll get lots of exposure here! Prices vary depending on whether you want a simple listing or a full showcase ad.

Marketing Resource #55: www.KwikPost.com is a nifty site that will syndicate your property listings to over twenty different real estate websites. This is a free service and proves to be a marvelous time saver!*

Marketing Resource #56: www.Postlets.com is a site that will automatically syndicate your real estate listings to a wide variety of social networking sites. This can be a real timesaver.

Marketing Resource #57: www.VFlyer.com calls itself the Web 2.0 "marketing toolbox" for online sellers. You'll find many tools here for creating imaginative, creative, professional-looking ads.

Marketing Resource Bonus? www.YouPriceIt.com is a simple free service like FSBO that allows you to create online flyers to post your deals.*

** Ad services are free of cost*

Online Real Estate Sites

The number of online sites where real estate can be bought and sold is vast and extensive. Realize that there are more of those sites than will fit within the scope of this or any book. Run various Google searches to find more. Any one of these might be exactly what you're looking for.

Social Networking

Marketing Resource #58: www.Facebook.com is the premier social networking site, and a great way to network. You could even start your own real estate investing group and invite others to join your group.

Marketing Resource #59: www.MySpace.com is very similar to Facebook, but doesn't perform all the same functions as Facebook. It is still a huge way to network around the globe.

Marketing Resource #60: ActiveRain.com is a social networking site geared toward real estate agents. The ActiveRain Real Estate Network is a free social network and marketing platform for real estate professionals. The network helps agents to create business relationships both within the industry and with the consumer. This is a great site to listen in on to see what's going on in the world of real estate and to perhaps make connections with an agent or two.

Marketing Resource #61: www.VirtualDealFactory.com is yet another site that serves as a social networking system for real estate investors. This is known as the "Facebook of Real Estate Investors," with daily training videos from the creators to do deals, and to meet buyers and friends. It's truly a place for ALL investors to meet and hang out and make more money. (Note: I am one of the creators of this site, and so I know firsthand how helpful this can be to a business.)

Online Networking

A look at online advertising would not be complete without discussing the subject of social networking. This concept is huge. You may have heard the term "Web 2.0." That simply refers to the vast opportunities online for viral growth and exposure. Social networking is a small part of the Web 2.0 scene. Many books have been written about social networking, but there is no way to exhaust the subject.

Social networking is not advertising in the strictest sense but, when it is understood and utilized correctly, it can result in a ton of fresh leads to your website.

How It Works

In order to make this clearer, let's compare it to a brick-and-mortar business. Say you own a shop on Main Street and the advertising you invest in includes such things as ads in the newspaper and on the local radio station, and a big ad in the local yellow pages. But you also attend every Chamber of Commerce function and there you mingle, shake hands, get to know the folks and hand out as many business cards as you can. That is comparable offline to what social networking is online.

Much of what you see on such sites such as Facebook and MySpace is hodge-podge and very sporadic. However, if done intentionally and purposefully (in order to build your leads list) it can be very beneficial for business.

While Facebook and MySpace were created prodominately for family and friends, they can still be utilized for the express purpose of promoting and showcasing your business and your talents and abilities—and the service you offer—in the field of real estate investing. No fees here—creating a profile is all free!

LinkedIn

Marketing Resource #62: Learn more about LinkedIn at www.LinkedIn.com. It's a great way to promote yourself and your business and it also lends a great deal of credibility. Here you can find answers to your questions about happenings in your industry.

Business Networking

LinkedIn is the business person's version of Facebook. It is not a place where you can purchase advertising per se. However, once you learn how to navigate this site you will be amazed at how fast you can build a growing network of professionals.

Creating a professional profile on LinkedIn adds a great degree of credibility to your business. It's certainly not difficult, although it will require a time investment at the outset.

This is a wonderful place to connect with a wide range of professionals. Here is where you might find a real estate agent in a city across the country where you are looking at a property, or where you might find an investor who is interested in finding rehabs in your town. Here you will also find many opportunities to set yourself apart as an expert in your field. The possibilities are endless.

LinkedIn offers many tutorials on the site, which will help you learn how to create your network and how to build a list of referrals.

Here's yet another way to give your URLs greater exposure. You will want to prominently display your Squeeze Pages and blog site addresses in your profile. Being a part of LinkedIn is a great way to get listed in major search engines as well.

Only you will know whether or not this kind of social networking is best for your particular business. It can't hurt to check it out.

Commenting On Blogs and Forums

Marketing Resource #63: www.MagicBullets.com is a national club site boasts a wide range of informative articles in addition to newsy forums. Here you can go in and learn or comment on the forums – or both.

Marketing Resource #64: On this site you will find a number of forums as well as blogs: www.InvestorsLoungeOnline.com

Marketing Resource #65: www.BiggerPockets.com/Forums is a great site for buyers and sellers both.

Increase Exposure

Another version of social networking is commenting on different blogs and forums. This is a great way to make your presence known. It's simple and it's free. It helps you to promote your own blog as well as to drive traffic to your Squeeze Pages.

The key here is not to become a pest, but add useful information to the forum or blog comments. Your knowledge of real estate will come into play here as you add tidbits of your own experiences in this industry. It's also a great way to connect with other investors.

Look on Google for "real estate investing blogs," making comments as you go. Because there is an endless supply of blogs and forums, choose only two or three and concentrate your efforts there. For forums, simply run a search on Google for "real estate investing forums."

By the way, this is yet another prime example of an activity that is easily farmed out. With a few simple instructions, you can hire an outsource person to make these posts for you (see Chapter 10).

Online Media Marketing

In Chapter 4, we took a close look at how to use videos to add life and sparkle to your online presence. However, working with videos is not the only venue for online media marketing. In this section we'll take a look at more options that are available to every real estate investor.

Teleconferencing (Conference Call)

Marketing Resource #66: www.FreeConferencePro.com is a free online service that will help you set up conference calls.

Marketing Resource #67: www.XIOSoftStore.com offers a $1 7-day trial. (Note: I personally use this service for my company.)

How Teleconferencing Works

Find a suitable teleconferencing program. E-mail your contacts and let them know about upcoming conference calls. You may want to conference with several of your investors and let them know the specifics of your newest bargain properties that are available. Such events lend great credibility to your business presence.

Technology and online services have made it extremely simple to set up a conference call with the possibility of receiving hundreds of listeners into the group. As you build your contact list, a teleconference call is a great way to quickly get word out about what you're offering as well as any upcoming special deals. Holding regularly scheduled conference calls sets you head and shoulders above your competition. Additionally, this is such a great way to share the message once with multiple people. This is yet another way to streamline the process and to work less and make more.

Webinars

Marketing Resource #68: www.GoToMeeting.com is a very popular, highly professional, site for providing webinar services. They offer a 30-day free trial and after that it is $99/month. (Note: I use this service in my own business.)

Marketing Resource #69: www.FuzeMeeting.com is comparable to GoToMeeting. They also offer a 30-day free trial.

Look Like An Expert

A webinar is a step up from a conference call. A webinar offers an online visual along with the audio. Webinars can be great teaching tools as you can implement a step-by-step power point presentation. As with conference calls, there are many different webinar providers and software. Take the time to call a few companies and discuss your needs.

By its very nature, webinars are more highly technical than a simple conference call. You will be tending to many more details. You will want to provide instructions that are easy to follow. Properly inform your attendees as to how to set up the needed programs and at the time the webinar will be held. The webinar provider you choose should help arrange these details.

The next step is to find a good polling service. This will help you to learn what your audience thought about the presentation and if they thought the instructions were simple to follow. What good is a webinar if you don't know what people thought of it?

Also attempt to learn what questions were not answered for your member via the webinar. This type of feedback will help you improve and streamline your approach. Polling and surveys help your attendees feel as though they are involved with the process. Someone who feels his or her opinion matters is more apt to respond better to what is presented.

What about cost? Webinar services range from free to those that come with a high price tag because they require special software and other applications such as dedicated servers. The route you choose will depend on what you are trying to get out of the webinar.

A free, or very low cost service, will not offer services such as support, troubleshooting, polling services, or archiving and recording services. These features alone may be important enough to justify the added expense. Keep in mind that some sites offer trials that allow you to test their service before committing to making a purchase. Bottom line, you must go with the service provider and the webinar style that will meet your needs.

In the end, professional webinars make you look like an expert in your field.

DVDs and CDs

Marketing Resource #70: Get creative by designing your own personalized DVDs and CDs. But make sure you use professional labeling and packaging to avoid the amateur look. Go here to see what's available: www.SuperMediaStore.com.

Use DVDs and CDs as Gifts and Freebies

It's so simple these days to create your own personalized DVDs and CDs. You create the information one time, put it on a DVD or CD, and give it away as a free gift. Now you have a fresh new marketing piece. Be imaginative and brainstorm for ideas to create select ones for your buyers, sellers, and investors.

If you offer the media pieces free on your Squeeze Pages, now you have a reason to ask for and to capture the physical mailing addresses of your various prospects. This greatly enhances your leads list.

Give them away as Christmas gifts, hand them out at trade fairs and business shows, or offer them as specials on your websites. The ideas are endless. And of course always make sure your Squeeze Page URL is featured both in the presentation and printed clearly on the labels and disc cases.

Offer useful information similar to the free special reports discussed in Chapter 9. This is one more way to expand your exposure and give you a professional stance.

Internet TV Shows

Marketing Resource #71: If producing and distributing your own online shows is in your future, you may want to look into www.Blip.tv as a starting place. They bill themselves as the "next-generation television network." BlipTV is focused on providing services to people who are making original Web shows for the Web. Their services include distribution, workflow automation and advertising sales service. BlipTV provides content creators with free hosting, support for a variety of video formats, distribution using technologies like RSS, and an opt-in advertising program with a 50/50 revenue share. BlipTV focuses on "episodic content" or "shows," as opposed to viral video. This is not a place to "advertise," but you can certainly disseminate information and make yourself known.

You Are the Star

Had you ever considered featuring your own online TV show (actually called a "web show")? You are the star of the show! You can invite guests and interview them and share newsy items from the real estate industry. If this is a new thought to you, I trust it's one you will seriously consider. What a great way to have your personality come across in a big way! As with many of the other technology-driven media marketing ideas, there are services to make this process simple and easy to follow.

While there are a number of avenues you can take to make this happen, BlipTV is probably the best.

Summary

As you can clearly see, the avenues, methods, and techniques for expanding your online presence are virtually endless. As you begin to incorporate more and more of these ideas into your marketing plan, you will soon have leads pouring in—more leads than you'll know what to do with. (But to learn exactly what to do with them, see Chapter 11.)
In the next chapter, we'll talk about your offline marketing plan and you get a in-depth perspective of how the two—your online and your offline marketing—can and should mesh together.

Chapter 8:
Marketing Offline

Does your family know that you're a real estate investor? How about your doctor? Your dentist? Hair stylist? Next door neighbor? I could go on and on, but you get the idea. This isn't the kind of business that is worked in your back bedroom on the computer in total seclusion. While we have discussed many tips for online marketing, remember that not every person you meet will be looking online. The best overall marketing strategy is to merge both online and offline advertising. Let everything you do offline, drive traffic to your Squeeze Pages. Your URL should appear in every ad and on every print piece you create.

The offline marketing ideas are numerous and widely varied. Hopefully, this list will spark your imagination and give you the impetus to get out there and get your name known.

Direct Mail

Marketing Resource #72: InfoUSA.com is an old standby in the direct mail industry. At this site you can learn more about direct mail as well as purchase mailing lists.

Marketing Resource #73: www.CactusMailing.com offers a wide range of services from printing to mailing.

Marketing Resource #74: At www.VistaPrint.com you'll find a site that offers a wealth of marketing tools, only one of which is direct mail services. (Look for "Postcard Marketing" under "Marketing Services" below.)

Direct Mail is Alive and Well

If you are one who thought that direct mailing was dead, think again. People still respond to pieces sent in the mail, especially if it is targeted specifically to their needs. However, do your research and enter into this marketing venue with great wisdom and more than a little restraint. You can throw away a lot of money quickly if this isn't done correctly.

If direct mail isn't part of your marketing mix, it may be time to re-evaluate. Direct mail allows you to target a specified group of prospects with personalized greetings and offerings. Direct mail allows you to control the quantities and costs of the mailing. It can be an economic advertising medium for those working on a tight budget.

Start Small

If you aren't really convinced of the viability of direct sales, why not take a small gamble and see if you can prove yourself wrong? A small, carefully crafted and targeted mailing can be an effective way to test the waters. The return on a small to medium-sized mailing can predict the results of a larger, more extensive mailing. If you get a disappointing return, use the failure to aid you in reworking your offering before sending it out to the masses.

Mailing Lists

After you've made the decision to take the direct mail route, your first step should be to contact a list broker. Supply the broker with a description of your service, goals and objectives, strategies, and target audience. The broker can assist you in selecting names based such things as location, age, gender, educational background, income level, interests, past purchasing patterns, credit history and more. By having a clear concept of your target audience, you can tailor the look and feel of the mail piece to match the prospect's age, gender, professional status, hobbies or any other desired criteria. (Contact the list brokers mentioned in the resources at the beginning of this section.)

Postcards

Keep in mind that direct mail doesn't have to be a letter inserted into an envelope. A postcard can be very effective, if not more so than a letter. When people receives a postcard in the mail, there's no need to open anything. It's in their hands and they are reading it before they even realize what they're doing. Not only do postcards demand instant attention, they are less costly to mail.

List Testing

List testing can teach you a lot about your customer base. A variety of offers can be sent to names from a single list. Conversely, a solitary proposition can be offered to names gathered from multiple lists. These tests will give you a clear and accurate accounting of who your best prospects are.

Quantifying Results

When introducing a new property, you will want to be able to measure the effectiveness of your direct mail campaign. It's easy to analyze the success of a direct mail effort, print, broadcast or online ad. You can measure the cost of your investment against the return.

Direct mail pieces are really targeted advertisements delivered directly to recipient's mailboxes. The success of your mailing is indicated by the initial flurry of first-time customers you gain as well as the number of customers who return again and again.

Yellow Pages

Marketing Resource #75: Listings.YellowPages.com. A nice display ad in the Yellow Pages is not cheap by any means. However, because it is in place for an entire year, it's one of those "set it and forget it" type of ads.

Yellow Pages: A Year-Long Ad

Anyone with a business phone line is automatically listed in the Yellow Pages. This is just a simple line listing.

However, since many entrepreneurs in today's market place use a cell phone only and don't have access that line listing, they will take out a display ad to magnify their marketing message.

Are Your Competitors There?

A good rule of thumb is to advertise in the Yellow Pages only if you see your competitors there. For many businesses, advertising in the Yellow Pages is the only way they market. Retailers and some service providers (like locksmiths, plumbers, restaurants, and hotels) rely on placement. However, if you get most of your business through referrals or other media, then you might want to pass.

The greatest benefit of a Yellow Pages ad is that, unlike other print ads, the prospect is searching with a distinct purpose in mind. Someone facing possible foreclosure would be overjoyed to see a Yellow Pages ad that says something like, "We Buy Houses; Walk Away Today; Instant Debt Relief; Fast Cash to You; We Pay Top Dollar." Always make sure to drive them to your site by offering a benefit, such as "Get a free report on how to stop foreclosure today."

Find Ways to Stand Out

Since your ad will be listed next to your competitors, you must find a way to stand out. Consider color if it's in the budget. If your competitors run large ads, you should too in order to avoid getting lost on the page. Use a strong headline to grab the reader's attention. Display the name of your company prominently, in a larger type size than your body copy. Also, be sure to identify the area you serve.

Contact information—phone number, physical address and Squeeze Page URL—should be in a larger type or of a bold color. Make it easy to be contacted. This is yet another great way to drive traffic to your website and build a list of targeted leads.

Write in personal style, listing the reasons people should do business with you. Briefly state what your business is about, then go on to list your benefits such as key services, and any incentives you offer. Use bullets and short phrases.

While the investment for a Yellow Pages ad is not cheap, it's an ad that never goes away. It is set in place for the coming year working for you while you are busy doing other things. Additionally, when someone finds you in the Yellow Pages, it's not an accident—they are looking for you. Those are the type of leads you are after.

Bandit Signs

Marketing Resource #76: www.AsaveALotSign.com is just one example of a site where you can get started using roadside (bandit) signs.

Marketing Resource #77: Another site offering great bargains on roadside signs is www.OakleySign.com. Here you will find a wide variety expressly for real estate investors.

Bandit Signs: An Effective Strategy

Bandit signs are the ugly-colored roadside signs put out to attract attention. The most common one for real estate investors says, "We Buy Houses." Of course they might also say, "For Sale By Owner," or "Why Rent?"

The term "bandit sign" came about because the signs are removed almost as soon as they are put out. And yet there are still a number of clever ways to make use of this strategy.

Place your signs in the yard of all your properties. Ask friends and neighbors if you can place a sign in their yards. Post them high on a utility pole so they are not easily removed.

(It is worth noting that some communities have stricter rules than others regarding the placement of signs. Some will administer fines for those who break the rules. Be aware of the ordinances in your particular city and act accordingly.)

Coroplast signs with wire stakes are the most weather resistant and easy to place. If you can't find a local sign maker, run a Google search and locate one online. I've given a couple resources here to get you started.

Many investors say that whenever business is slow, they simply take the time to put out about 25 to 50 roadside signs that feature their contact number and URL, and the leads start rolling in.

Place roadside signs at strategic intersections to attract leads. Signs that are put out on Friday and are in place during the weekend receive the most exposure. These can be used to bring either buyers or sellers or investors, depending on the wording of the sign.

Real Estate Agents

Marketing Resource #78: Use this site to begin your search for a local agent to work with: www.Connect2Agent.com
Marketing Resource #79: www.HomesAndLand.com is yet another site with many listings in your specific area with many realtor contacts.

Keep Searching for an Agent

You've perhaps heard that real estate agents and real estate investors are at odds with one another. Or perhaps you have actually experienced this firsthand. But don't be too quick to dismiss these agents. Who in your community knows more about what's going on in the area of real estate? The key here is persistence. Keep searching until you find the right agent who is willing to work in partnership with you.

Exchange Leads

You will have individuals in your contact list who are not at all comfortable with your creative financing methods. These leads can go to your agent friend. Likewise, the agent will have the names of people who cannot qualify for conventional loans, or people who are looking to buy directly from an investor. Those leads could come to you. You might also gain access to the names of "expired listings." This list of frustrated home sellers is exactly what you need!

These are just a few examples of how an understanding, cooperative agent can benefit your business. This agent may also know the names of other professionals in the field with whom you can be connected.

So don't give up. Keep seeking until you find the agent (or agents) who sees the rewards of this type of strong relationship.

Mortgage Broker

Marketing Resource #80: Seek out a mortgage broker who understands and is in sympathy with the workings of a real estate investor. Partner with this person to exchange both leads and information. You can find the name of a mortgage broker from your local network or with a directory site like www.PersonalHomeLoanMortgages.com/broker.

As with real estate agents, it is highly beneficial to have a mortgage broker on your "professional team." This is a great source for leads, as well as connecting with other professionals. Take all the time necessary to find the broker who wants to work in partnership with your real estate investing skills.

Property Managers

Marketing Resource #81: Take the time to meet and get to know several property managers and exchange information with them. You can start with this directory site: www.PropertyManagementFinder.com.

Property managers are often in close relationship with landlords and may know of a few "frustrated" ones who ware looking to dump unwanted properties. Likewise, these managers are familiar with some of the better local contractor teams around town. Don't overlook this great resource. Call on several of these businesses in your community and make friends. It will pay off in the end.

Chamber of Commerce

Marketing Resource #82: Check out your local Chamber of Commerce at www.ChamberOfCommerce.com. Join the Chamber if possible, and become an active, involved member. At the very least, get a schedule of the Chamber's activities and attend as many functions as you can. Most Chambers hold regular meetings and get-togethers such as business fairs. Some sponsor small business network groups that meet weekly for lunch or breakfast.

What a great opportunity to "meet and greet" those in your community! Keep in mind that most everyone, sooner or later, is either buying a home or selling one—or they know someone who is. When you're out among the people, it increases your chances to find the deals.

Flyers

Marketing Resource #83: www.MyFlyerGuys.com
Marketing Resource #84: www.AllDelivered.com

In this day of high tech few people even think of how effective a flyer can be. However, five hundred or a thousand brightly colored flyers delivered to homes in a carefully selected neighborhood can reap great rewards. Design a simple informational flyer explaining that you buy house (or have one designed for you). Keep in mind that door-hangers are also effective.

This is definitely an outsource job. You can find such services as flyer distribution in your local Yellow Pages. See the resources listed in this section. Or, if you are just beginning and your budget is small, hire a few teenagers to do the footwork for you. Just be sure they are reliable and trustworthy.

The flyer can let people know that you are looking to buy homes in that neighborhood. This is a great way to get calls coming in, or to drive more traffic to your Squeeze Pages. And it's definitely a great way to get your name out there. At a relatively low cost, this marketing strategy can pay off big time.

Be sure to prominently display your contact information, especially your Squeeze Page URL. One deal will more than pay for this cheap mode of advertising. And think of the exposure!

Bulletin Boards

Marketing Resource #85: Utilize all local bulletin boards you can find. Brainstorm to come up with half a dozen public places where your brightly colored informational flyers can be posted. Then hire someone to post them for you on a regular basis.

Think of public gathering places, such as Laundromats, and make use of their bulletin boards by posting your flyers. Some investors go to large apartment buildings and ask for permission to post flyers on their bulletin boards. If you are offering rent-to-own properties (or lease option properties), an apartment building is where your key prospects are living. This is a simple, inexpensive, and effective way to let the public know.

At the bottom of the flyer, have tear-off tabs containing your Squeeze Page URL and phone number. Again, this is not high-tech stuff. But you are after people, and this is where people gather.

Business Cards

Marketing Resource #86: Have business cards printed giving your name, business name, logo, contact information, and Squeeze Page URL. Hand them out wherever you go. If you are just starting out and money is tight, begin with free business cards from www.VistaPrint.com. [Note: Please invest the money to have the Vista Print logo removed from the back of the cards. If not, it shows that you are not serious about your business. It says, "I'll buy your house for thousands of dollars but I will not invest 5 bucks to take off the Vista Print logo."]

A Business Card is Your *Representative*

When attending networking events, always make sure you have a fistful of business cards. They aren't doing you any good in the box in your desk drawer. Get them out into people's hands.

You may start out with inexpensive (or free) business cards; however, as soon as you can afford it, invest in cards that are professionally designed and printed. That card is your representative. Make it work effectively!

One other note about business cards—use the back of the card. Why waste that empty space? The back of your card can work like a tiny billboard. Get specific about the benefits of your services and make them known.

If pennies are still scarce and you are just starting out, you may want to check out www.VistaPrint.com where you can get a box of "starter" business cards for free by using one of their templates.

Letterhead

Marketing Resource #87: www.VistaPrint.com offers a wide variety of templates under the "real estate" theme to create personalized letterhead and thank you cards. Or, use their resources to create your own design.

Add a Professional Touch

While it's true that not many letters are written these day (E-mail is king) it's still important for you to have professional letterhead sporting your business logo—and this logo should match your business cards. Your letterhead is yet another place where you can publish your Squeeze Page URL as well as your blog.

I know investors who also have matching thank you cards printed. They make sure that after every deal is closed, each person who took part in the deal receives a personal, hand-written thank you card. Such a personal touch goes a long way in building good relationships. And the professional look of the card further enhances your credibility! Need I add that your contact information and website URL will be on the thank you cards as well?

Calendars

Marketing Resource #88: In late summer or early fall, invest in having personalized calendars printed that give all the pertinent information about your company. www.VistaPrint.com offers a wide variety of designs. Give these calendars as Christmas gifts to all your business contacts and keep your name before their eyes all year long. Here's a great way to keep your name in front of your prospects all year long.

Promotional Materials

Marketing Resource #89: www.PromosOnTime.com offers a wide variety of promotional items—everything from mugs, to key chains, to tote bags, to ball caps, to personalized pads of sticky notes.

Marketing Resource #90: www.GoPromos.com

Marketing Resource #91: www.CafePress.com also features many promotional items.

Promotional Materials: Mobile Advertising

Ever sign a contract and have someone give you a pen with his or her name and contact information on it? Or have you ever gone to a trade fair and come away with a bag full of mugs, key chains, pens, and pads of sticky notes? Promotional materials are items you may want to look into as your business grows.

As with the calendars mentioned in the previous Marketing Resource, such promotional materials provide effective ways to increase exposure and keep your name and contact information in the public eye. The person who has your personalized coffee mug sitting on his desk, is much more likely to call you when he is faced with unloading an unwanted property.

Television

Marketing Resource #92: Once your business is up and running, you may want to consider creating a professional television ad. If you have created an E-book or a free special report, these can be offered through your ad. And, of course, your Squeeze Page URL will be prominently displayed, as well as mentioned several times. Check prices at www.NationalTVSpots.com.

Television Offers Affordable, Effective Advertising

Television time is less expensive than ever. It can also be more effective than ever if you understand it. While it's true that people are spending more time with their PCs and cell phones, it's also true that the lines between them all are blurring. Television deserves a place in the arsenal of a small business now more than ever.

The main reasons why this is true are because 1) television now allows you to target your audience more precisely than you could in the past; 2) television lets you single out specific groups of people, such as business people; and 3) it enables you to hone in on selected neighborhoods in your community. These phenomena are due to the growth of cable TV.

Television is now more affordable than it ever has been, in many cases lower in cost than radio. Direct response companies are discovering this by the dozens and are also discovering there is a 24-hour viewing audience out there and that there are program-length infomercials that cost what regular one-minute spots used to cost. Again, we tip our hats to the cable industry for putting TV advertising within the reach of everyone. (See the sidebar *Ten Tips for Television Marketing*.)

Ten Tips for Television Advertising

1. Television is inexpensive. The cost to run commercials is no more than $20 during prime-time in most markets in the United States. The cost to *produce* a commercial should run you no more than $1000. You no longer need some big-name star to endorse what you have to offer. Remember, you're after sales, not an Emmy.

2. Television is a visual medium. Don't think of it as a radio spot with pictures. Think of it as a visual story with a beginning, a middle, and an end. Because over 70% of us mute the commercials with our remotes, if you're not giving your story and your name visually, you're not telling your story or saying your name at all.

3. Television is powered by an idea. Forget the special effects, music, staging and lighting. First think of the idea. That's what makes a commercial successful—a strong offer, a visual expression of a good idea. Once you have the idea, everything else will fall into place. Without the idea, your commercial has hardly any chance of success.

4. Television is made fascinating by special effects. Many people get carried away at their opportunities to be like Steven Spielberg and fall prey to gizmos and gimmicks. Use special effects to highlight your idea, to focus on your idea, to further your idea and then you'll see why they're so special. Otherwise, they act like vampires, sucking attention away from your offer with their dazzle.

5. Television doesn't cost as little as you think. There I was telling you right off the bat that TV is inexpensive, and here I am, one minute later, telling you that it's not so inexpensive. It's true that the spots are inexpensive. It's also true that the production can be inexpensive. But you've got to run several spots every day, several days a week, three weeks out of four, and for a minimum of three months—unless you're making a direct response offer—before you see any glimmerings of proof that TV is doing the job for you. If you're looking for instant gratification, look somewhere other than the tube.

6. **Television is made better if you operate from a script**. You need not waste your precious money having somebody produce a storyboard for you because you don't need one. But you do need a script that tells the exact visuals and the exact sounds that will go on for 30 seconds.

7. Television production costs are lower if when you pre-produce with care. The way to cut thousands of dollars from your TV production costs is by have pre-production meetings where all production details are handled. These are followed by rehearsals for the talent and the technicians. There should be zero surprises on the day of the TV shooting.

8. Television production costs are lowered still if you produce your sound track first. After you've got it, you can shoot footage to match the amount of time the words and music take. Shooting sound and picture at the same time means that if a plane flies overhead or a truck drives by, you've got to re-shoot. Do your sound first, using professionals, then shoot the visuals.

9. Television's greatest strength is its ability to demonstrate. As newspapers give the news and magazines involve readers, as radio provides intimacy and direct response adds urgency, television's power is the way it can demonstrate. It can show before and after, with a shot of the product in use during the middle. It can hit left and right-brained people. It can combine all the art forms into a masterful blending of show and sell.

10. Television is still the undisputed heavyweight champion of marketing. I love online marketing so much that I'm nearly bursting with enthusiasm for it. I know it's going to make every other medium stronger and more effective.

But you'll find that television can talk directly to your specific target audience and that it will cost you much less than you figured. And, if you've got the patience to commit to a TV campaign, you're going to be delighted at how it rewards your patience. Plus, it is a great way to drive traffic to your Internet website.

A final word: Just as being online doesn't mean beans unless it's part of a well-crafted marketing program, being on television is also no guarantee of profitability unless it is part of a program and supported with other media.

Word-of-Mouth and Referrals

Marketing Resource #93: Never leave referrals and Word-of-Mouth to chance. Learn practical ways to cultivate this area of your marketing plan. Word-of-Mouth is extremely powerful, and is relatively cost-free. Always keep in mind that W-O-M doesn't stand alone, but works in tandem with other marketing venues.

Word-of-Mouth Doesn't Just Happen

Because of the rapid growth of viral marketing online, Word-of-Mouth advertising can, in today's marketplace, happen both online and offline. Contrary to popular belief, Word-of-Mouth advertising doesn't just happen. You have to generate it yourself. Too many entrepreneurs believe that simply providing an excellent product or service is enough to catapult people to their door (or website).

Marketing plans based on Word-of-Mouth (W-O-M) require an understanding of the "science" of purchasing decisions. Think about a business that you yourself have recommended and consider what aspects inspired this endorsement.

Negative W-O-M Travels Fast

People tend to share their disappointment rather than their satisfaction. Your customers are no different. Although great customer service can't hurt your business, it is more likely to *decrease negative* W-O-M than significantly *increase positive* W-O-M.

Always respond immediately to negative W-O-M that comes to your attention. Determine whether it was slander cast by an unreasonable customer, or a competitor, and respond calmly with a solid point-by-point defense. When customers come to you with a complaint, do what you can to send them away happy. Negative feelings occur in a heartbeat, but can linger for years if they are not dealt with immediately. Let your customers know that they can bring their complaints to you.

Don't Forget to Ask

Train yourself to ask for two things every time you close a deal: a positive testimony, and names and contact information of others who may need your services.

One of the best methods of building W-O-M is through testimonials. Testimonials are easy to understand and relate to, and they allow prospects to visualize using your product. You can solicit formal letters and E-mails. If you overhear a passing compliment or recommendation from a customer, request permission to quote them. Always get authorization before using the quotations and maintain a file in case you need to verify the source.

Make every effort to collect customer interactions that depict your company's honesty and integrity. Share these stories generously in brochures, newspaper, radio and television advertising, direct mail pieces, newsletters, on your Squeeze Pages and blog site, and in personal correspondence with customers.

Like any other promotional methods, W-O-M will not stand alone. The success will result from a combination of marketing efforts. What appears to be Word of Mouth advertising, is often a combination of newspaper, magazine, radio, direct-mail, online, *and* Word-of-Mouth.

Public Speaking

Marketing Resource #94: If you are considering public speaking as part of your marketing strategies, you may want to look into becoming part of a local Toastmasters International club (www.Toastmasters.org). Weekly (or bi-weekly) club meetings offer a non-threatening setting in which to learn not only speaking skills, but leadership skills as well. There are nominal dues assessed every six months; however, you are welcome to visit a few times before deciding if you want to join.

Marketing Resource #95: Attend local church functions. Contact several local churches and offer to bring a presentation of interest such as "How to Avoid Foreclosure," or "How to Buy a Home Using Creative Financing." Give a free gift of printed copies of your special report (Chapter 2), or your DVDs and CDs (Chapter 7). Or, you can also opt to offer one-on-one consultations with interested persons at the close of the meeting. This same tactic will work just as well with civic groups.

Marketing Resource #96: Become familiar with your local media outlets. Call up your local television and/or radio station and get to know the people there. Explore the possibility of taking part in a live interview. Use your knowledge of the business to offer much-needed information. Learn to think creatively; think outside the box.

Realize that Public Speaking is a Learned Talent

Public speaking is rather like writing in that you may feel you have no skill or ability in this field. However, it is a talent that can absolutely be learned. The wonderful thing about public speaking is that your personality is totally involved. While the print medium (and even your website) offers a limited scope of who you are, public speaking opens the door even further. Once you connect favorably with an audience, you now have a new group of "fans" who will want to do business with you.

If this is an area you would like to explore, consider joining a local Toastmasters International club. There are always several clubs in every community. Not only will you learn speaking skills, but it's another great place to network and get yourself known.

Many doors will open to you once you feel comfortable at a podium. You can conduct your own seminars, offer your speaking services to church and civic groups, create your own infomercials, and line up interview sessions on television and radio spots.

Sponsor a Charity Event

Marketing Resource #97: Join in with other merchants to support a charity event, or create and promote an event on your own. It is a great way to become involved in the community while gaining positive publicity.

Support Your Favorite Charity

Do you have a favorite charity? Most people do. Is there going to be a community-wide event promoting that charity in which you can become an active part? This is an effective way to become known within your community and be of service at the same time. Your company name and logo will appear in flyers, programs, bulletins, or perhaps even large banners that are used for the event.

Or you may want to create an event on your own and invite other merchants and business people to take part. This could be anything from a raffle, to a banquet, to a pancake breakfast, to a golf tournament. It takes a great deal of planning for such events, but is highly rewarding on many levels.

If it becomes an annual event, your company will always be associated with it. Again, you are supporting a worthy cause and creating positive publicity at the same time. Such events are definitely newsworthy and will be a great subject for a press release (see Chapter 6).

Open House

Marketing Resource #98: Hold open houses on a regular basis to show off the properties you have available. Use the event to increase your exposure in the area, plus add fresh new names to your growing leads list.

Show Off Your Properties

Real estate agents do it—why can't you? Do what? Hold an open house. It's a great way to show off one of your investment properties. You can advertise, put the flags and signs out, distribute flyers in the neighborhood, and place ads in the neighborhood newspapers.

On Open House Day, make sure you have plenty of business cards on hand, as well as flyers that give all the particulars of the home and how it can be acquired. Don't try to handle this event on your own. Have someone stationed at the front door to greet visitors and capture their contact information, and to make sure they are handed available materials. This leaves you free to converse with visitors and answer all their questions.

If you are offering a lease option or rent-to-own on your properties, make that clear as so many families today are unable to acquire funding through the traditional channels. That fact alone should draw a large number of interested people.

Try not to let anyone leave without getting his or her contact information. This adds to your growing list of leads. Tell them, "This home may not meet your needs, but we have several a month come available. I'd like to be able to E-mail you this information on a regular basis."

If they are even mildly serious about purchasing a home, they'll be glad to get the updated information. (You can also outsource this to your local team as well.)

Bus Tours

Marketing Resource #96: As your inventory of below-market, fixer-uppers grows, consider setting up a bus tour to make quick work of the flips. If you haven't the resources to rent a bus, start with a large van and grow from there.

Move Properties Quickly

As your business continues to grow, and your inventory of investment-type properties grows, you will be looking for more creative ways in which to move them quickly.

Many people today are looking for cheap houses to rehab to use as rentals or as their own homes. This search is no longer limited to the ones you normally think of as those investing in real estate as an ongoing vocation. These are your buyer prospects and their numbers are increasing daily.

Because these numbers are growing, you might consider setting up a bus tour to showcase your “bargains” that you have available. What a great way to sell several properties in one fell swoop.

Announce well in advance that your tours are for serious buyers only. You are not looking for curiosity seekers or tire-kickers. Proof of Funds letters or Pre-Approval Letters from a viable hard moneylender must be faxed or emailed or there will be no access to the tour. Use the scarcity technique by saying you expect there to be a waiting list.

Accept Bids on the Spot

There are many ways to handle the tour itself. If you are looking to create a sense of urgency accept the bids on the spot. The investors will love it.

Supply each tour member with an information sheet and bid sheet for each property. Silent bids will be taken upon the visit of each property and the winning bid announced before proceeding to the next stop. An earnest money deposit will be required from each buyer.

You may not have the wherewithal to start such an undertaking with a huge bus, but it’s pretty simple to rent a large van. Start small and think big. The more deals you turn, and the quicker you turn them, the more your profit margin grows!

Bird Dogs

Marketing Resource #97: If you are in the wholesaling area of real estate investing (which you should always be in one way or another) market for someone to be your bird dog—someone to sniff out the deals. You will then be free to invest your time in activities that make money, such as negotiating the deals. Check at a great free resource for you over at: www.VirtualBirdDogDeals.com, and sign up to receive the ten lessons that will show you how to educate your bird dogs the right way.

Start with One Bird Dog and Work Up

This is one job you should definitely consider outsourcing. Those who "sniff out" such great wholesale deals have been nicknamed by other investors as "bird dogs."

When looking for your bird dog, you will want someone who has his or her own transportation, who possibly wants to learn more about the real estate investing business, and has a flexible schedule. This could be a college student, or a retired senior citizen, or a single mom.

You will map out an area in which your bird dog will locate properties for you. They will take photos and fill out a fact sheet (that you provide) for each prospective investment property they find. (See the sample forms included at the back of this book.)

How you pay your bird dog is up to you, but most investors pay up to $500 for each property they are able to acquire and flip. Because bird dogs are paid on the finished sale, they will become more and more adept at sniffing out the best deals.

Once your cash flow is ramped up, you may want to take on two or three more. Or, why wait? They only get paid when you buy and sell, so get as many as you can. Soon you'll have enough properties to substantiate the need for a bus tour as described in the Marketing Resource above.

Billboards

Marketing Resource #98: There may come a point in your growing business when highway billboards will be the perfect medium to get your message across. Billboards and other forms of outdoor advertising can be highly effective and efficient. What a way to capture a lot of attention on a consistent basis! You can start your research right now at www.OutdoorBillboard.com.

A Billboard is Just *There*

Perhaps you've wondered about this marketing marvel as you've driven down the highway and had a particular billboard catch your eye. Billboards have been a part of the American landscape for decades.

Like a Yellow Pages ad, a billboard is there for months at a time, unlike TV or newspaper ads that are here today and gone tomorrow. A billboard cannot be turned off or put down. It's just *there.*

Because of today's computer technology, billboards are designed on a computer screen, printed to vinyl or poster paper, and glued to the billboard structure. This results in higher quality ads in less time for less money.

(And have you seen the latest digital billboard? They have the look of a TV or computer screen. At this time, these are the priciest, so you probably won't want to start with them, but they are effective in some cases.)

Cost

The cost of a billboard runs from around $700 a month to over $2,000. When you factor in how many pairs of eyes will see your ad—on a daily basis as they are driving to and from wherever—it's really a bargain. One or two deals would more than pay for it.

It's important to remember this is a visual medium, not text! Just a few descriptive words are needed—words to paint a picture in the mind of the reader. Study billboards and make notes on the ones that, in your opinion, actually work, and what ones do not.

Other Types of Billboards

You might also consider other types of *billboard* advertising such as wrap-around ads on a local bus, signs inside buses and taxis, in airports, bus depots, and restaurants. You may even consider a wrap-around paint ad for your own vehicle that you use on a daily basis for your investing business.

As with all the other marketing strategies discussed in this book, billboard advertising should be only one part of an ongoing, growing plan. It's definitely not a stand-alone promotion.

Summary

Just because Internet marketing is inexpensive and highly effective is not a reason to leave offline marketing in the lurch. Both can work together. Use all your offline marketing venues to work to funnel traffic to your Squeeze Pages and your blog site. Both together are stronger than either one standing alone.

Memorize These 12 Words, Then Live By Them

Run your business by the marketing concepts contained in these twelve words and you'll soon be in *marketing heaven*.

1. **Commitment**: You should know that a mediocre marketing program with commitment will always prove more profitable than a brilliant marketing program without commitment. Commitment makes it happen.

2. **Investment**: Marketing is not an expense, but an investment—the best investment available in America today—if you do it right. With this book to guide you, you'll be doing it right.

3. **Consistent**: It takes a while for prospects to trust you and if you change your marketing, media, and identity, you're hard to trust. Restraint is a great ally of the successful marketer. Repetition is another.

4. **Confident**: In a nationwide test to determine why people buy, price came in fifth, selection fourth, service third, quality second, and, in first place, people said they patronize businesses in which they are confident.

5. **Patience**: Unless the person running your marketing is patient (that may be you!), it will be difficult to practice commitment. View marketing as an investment, be consistent, and make prospects confident. Patience is a marketer's virtue.

6. **Assortment**: Successful marketers know that individual marketing weapons rarely work on their own. But marketing combinations do work. A wide assortment of marketing tools is required to woo and win customers.

7. **Convenient**: People now know that time is not money, but is far more valuable. Respect this by being easy to do business with and running your company for the convenience of your customers, not yourself.

8. **Subsequent**: The real profits come after you've made the sale, in the form of repeat and referral business. Those who fail to grow their businesses think marketing ends when they've made the sale. Successful marketers know that's when marketing begins.

9. **Amazement**: There are elements of your business that you take for granted, but prospects would be amazed if they knew the details. Be sure all of your marketing always reflects that amazement. It's always there.

10. **Measurement**: You can actually double your profits by measuring the results of your marketing. Some weapons hit bulls-eyes. Others miss the target. Unless you measure, you won't know which is which.

11. **Involvement**: This describes the relationship between you and your customers—and it *is* a relationship. You prove your involvement by following up; they prove theirs by patronizing and recommending you.

12. **Dependent**: The guerrilla's job is not to compete but to cooperate with other businesses. Market them in return for them marketing you. Set up tie-ins with others. Become dependent to market more, spend less.

Chapter 9:
Special Reports Equal More Money

Marketing Resource #99: Create Special Reports and give them away to draw prospects to your website and capture their contact information. This increases exposure, builds trust, and grows your leads list.

Tap Into the Power

When you hear the phrase "special report," what comes to mind? Do you think that it is a report so *special* and so in depth that it can only be written by a college professor or a published author? Do you cross it off your list because you don't think of yourself as having the authority or the ability to write a special report? If up to this point you have totally discounted using special reports, ask yourself why. Then take a minute to explore the many reasons why you *should* tap into the power of this simple marketing tool.

Let's say you are trying to attract a new buyer for your home and yet you are not getting as many eyes on your property as you would like. Consider this solution.

Simple Method

Create a report that answers the top ten questions that all buyers have. If you are not sure exactly what those questions might be, call a couple of real estate agents and ask them.

If you don't relish the idea of calling agents and asking them for information, then simply log in to the "billion dollar information bank" known as Google.com. Type in a few questions and use the answers to compile this special report.

Now begin to think of catchy title possibilities, such as:

- The Top 10 Questions To Ask Before Buying Your New Home
- The Top 10 FAQ's All Soon-To-Be Homeowners Need to Ask
- 10 Crucial Questions You Must Ask Before Buying Your Next Home

See how simple this can be? Since you have already started your marketing system by building your websites and Squeeze Pages, now you have the perfect place to offer your free report. Of course, the site visitor will have to enter their name and email address in order to receive that free report. (This is how you build a great list.)

The word "free" is one of the strongest words that can be used in marketing. People are drawn to *free*. And once they receive that free gift from you, they now feel a connection with you. Especially if you allow a bit of your personality to shine through the report.

Outsource the Writing

I'm continually surprised at how few real estate investors make use of this simple and yet highly effective marketing tool.

Perhaps you're reading this and thinking, "I don't like to write. I'm not a good at writing. I don't have time to write." And on and on. You don't have to be a writer to create special reports. Actually, I'm not a very good writer either. And I certainly am limited on the time to spend writing. But I certainly know how to outsource (see Chapter 10). There are many good writers who are willing and ready to write for you. You come up with the ideas and let that "hired pen" implement the project for you. Never let a list of excuses stop you from moving forward with your marketing plan.

Which Would You Choose?

Consider this: Say you were shopping for a house, and you see two ads. One of those ads says, "Contact me to buy a house." The second one says, "Contact me to get a *free special report* on buying a new home." Which one would you call? Between the two it might be a tossup. In fact, you might contact both of them.

So, now you get in contact with both of these investors who are selling properties. Investor number one simply tries to sell their property. Investor number two, on the other hand says, "Thanks for calling. To get your special report get on over to www.YourSqueezePage.com where you can quickly and easily access your free report."

The investor who takes this route of giving a free gift is far more likely to make a sale (and build a strong buyer list) than the investor who does not. This giving of a free gift opens the door for a non-threatening introduction between the buyer and seller. In the act of receiving the free gift, the potential buyer has warmed up to the seller. In addition, that potential buyer is being educated in exactly how to purchase a property.

Leads List

As I mentioned at the beginning of this book, all of the resources offered here are designed to increase the flow of leads that come into your "marketing funnel."

When you offer your free report on your Squeeze Page or blog site, your visitor must enter in their email address and name into your Squeeze Page in order to receive this gift. As more and more people request this report, your list grows and grows.

Permission Marketing

Can you see how and why this works so well? You may just have a property that you are in the process of selling; or you may know someone who has a property for sale and you are the middleman. You are putting the deal together and finding the buyer—better known as *wholesaling*. Whatever the situation, you are capturing leads and making friends.

This kind of marketing is known as Permission Marketing. It is a well-known marketing technique in the business world. It is based on the premise that people prefer to do business with someone they know, trust and like. With this in mind, you can see why it's so important to get something in the hands of your prospects that has your name, your company name, your website link (a link that will show the properties you are offering).

Once you start implementing this kind of strategy, you will definitely separate yourself from the crowd.

Summary

So, if creating special reports works so well, then why isn't everyone doing this? It's simple. Many people are lazy. But you refuse to be. Some people never get it. But you do. Some people believe there must be a secret formula and they must wait until they find it.

There *is* a simple formula—it's called "Just do it!"

If you are grabbing hold of the value of special reports and you are ready to move forward, we have created several reports that are available at low cost. The work has already been done for you and you are set to go! Go to www.InvestorSpecialReports.com.

Chapter 10:
Outsourcing – Key to Exponential Growth

Marketing Resource #100: www.Elance.com is one of the premier sites online to find professional and semi-professional freelancers. Before hiring anyone, you have access to their profile, their education and professional accomplishments, as well as feedback from other clients. In other words, you will know the person you are working with.
Marketing Resource #101: www.Guru.com is very similar to Elance. Here you will find qualified freelancers from around the globe. Once you realize how simple it is to find and hire quality people, you'll wonder why you waited so long. Strong working relationships are built in this environment and often last for many years.

Outsource Your Busy Work

In this chapter, I hope to give you a total paradigm shift in your thinking with regard to how you operate your real estate investing business on a day-to-day basis. In order to change your mindset, you must first become completely and totally convinced that your time is valuable. Too valuable to be dealing with mundane tasks that amount only to busy work. As one person put it, "jobs that are equal to straightening the chairs on the deck of the Titanic." In other words, tasks of no lasting consequence.

Create your own "Worth Chart." Think of the amount that you would like to earn in a year, or per month. Now break it down to calculate what your hourly "fee" comes to. With this as your guide, you will have a clearer perspective of just how much your time is worth.

At the end of the day, have you been involved only in activities that are income-generating? Or have you inundated yourself with tasks that anyone could do? You are the one who should be negotiating deals and closing deals, attending closings and taking checks to the bank. Only you can answer these questions. I suggest you begin to keep a log of what tasks you undertake each day, then place a check mark beside every one that could be outsourced. Notice I didn't say which ones you could *afford* to outsource but which ones *could* be outsourced.

Where to Begin

At first, when your business is small and struggling, you will be forced by necessity to take care of most all the details. But don't get in the habit. Make it a goal to begin to outsource just as soon as your budget allows.

Begin with the smaller tasks such as finding and commissioning a bird dog. That same person may be the one who could set out your roadside signs. After all, they're out and about anyway.

As your business grows you will begin seeking out an administrative assistant to post your blogs, place online ads, comment on forums and the like. You may also want to hire a writer to create your blogs, articles, press releases, autoresponder letters and newsletters.

Creating a Lifestyle

If you thought outsourcing was only for big corporations, think again. The entire scene, in this sense, has drastically changed. In today's global marketplace, at the click of a mouse you can find highly qualified individuals to accomplish a myriad of tasks for you. Remember, you are not in real estate investing simply to create another full-time job for yourself. You are looking to create a lifestyle where your time is your own.

Think about it. The more time you can spend working on lucrative deals, the more money you will make. The more money you make the more your business grows and the more you can afford to outsource the work. Your goal here is to have more time to spend the way *you* want to spend it.

Finding Providers

There are many sites online where you can find such professionals. My three favorites are www.Elance.com, www.Guru.com and www.Craigslist.com. Here you will post the job or project you want done. Providers on those sites will bid on the job. You are free to choose which one you will take. In other words, you are naming your own price. This way you are assured of always staying within your budget.

Whether you find people online or in your own community is not important. What is important is that you have enough respect for yourself not to waste your time, your talents, or your energy on dead-end tasks that are not generating streams of income.

Never be satisfied with your business until you are outsourcing every task that is not directly related to cash-generating activities. The more you outsource, the freer your mind and your time will be. Your stress levels will be greatly diminished. Once you grasp this concept and begin to incorporate it, you will soon see massive exponential growth in your business and, hence, in your income.

Summary

The key to conducting a strong, growing business is learning to delegate. Can you imagine the president of a large corporation working in the assembly line of the company? How could such a company run efficiently?

Quite literally, you are the CEO of your own company and your life, and you must see yourself in that light. When you do, you will step up into a higher level of business growth.

Chapter 11:
Setting Your Business in Order

What to do With Business Leads?

As I work with real estate investors around the country on a regular basis, the one cry I hear the most is the need for an ongoing supply of quality leads. Everyone is looking for more leads.

But the question I have for these investors is this: If I gave you a thousand (1,000) real estate buyer leads today, what would you do with them? Do you have systems in place to take care of them?

Take a few minutes and answer these questions regarding incoming leads:

1. How do you manage them?
2. How do you get the most value out of them?
3. How do you avoid the tire kickers as much as possible?
4. How do you make money off of them without EVER talking to them?
5. How do you find the deals?

This is more important than many investors realize. What good is an endless supply of leads if there is no system in place to manage them? Without systems, you will quickly crash and burn.

You Need a System

www.VirtualRealEstateWebsites.com exists for just this reason. These pages are already done for you, showing you that Squeeze Pages coupled together with autoresponder letters offer a number of ways for leads to be processed quickly and easily.

In Chapter 10, we talked about the need for outsourcing a number of mundane tasks that steal your time and lower your efficiency (and your profit margin). Now think of your Squeeze Pages and other technology-based helps as yet another way to "outsource." Let the automated systems work for you.

When a potential home seller visits your site and sees that your services are a viable option, that visitor will leave his or her name and E-mail address, possibly to get that free report you're offering. (By the way, you also get Buyer, Seller, and Investor reports with this amazing service.) That contact information goes directly to your autoresponder account and your pre-written E-ails begin going out to that person immediately. That "dripping" will continue for as long as you have the E-mails set up to do so.

You may never need to talk to that prospect until he or she is truly serious enough to give you a phone call, or send a personal E-mail asking for an appointment. Think of the time and effort saved. Not to mention eliminating the stress of talking to half-interested tire-kickers.

Learn to Work Smart

The key to your successful business is for you to work smart and not hard. You must have a process by which you weed out all but the most serious "lookers." Streamline your business with www.VirtualRealEstateWebsites.com.

You may not be a computer whiz—and I can tell you I am certainly not—but some of the best in the business set up this system. Through VirtualRealEstateWebsites, you get services such as ongoing professional training, pre-written E-mails to use in your autoresponder, and the same profit-generating techniques that I use in my own business, just to name a few. There's more. Lots more.

All of this is offered at a fraction of the cost that it used to be when first offered to investors. And since you have this book in your hands, you are getting the $599 set-up fee waived. In addition, you will be getting a free course that's worth $897 that will expand on the easiest way to make money in real estate without risking it all—our way to say, "Thank you." It is definitely affordable for any investor who is looking to grow their business in a big way.

This book was designed to give you a wide range of marketing ideas and a wide range of mediums. But all the marketing in the world will do you no good if you aren't fully prepared to take care of the responses that are sure to come from those advertising venues. Check out the simple system offered to by www.VirtualRealEstateWebsites.com. You will be so thankful that you did.

Final Words

"You don't have to get it right
You just have to get it going"

Pick a couple of the tools outlined in this book and go implement as quickly as humanly possible. It is very crucial to successful entrepreneurs that they take fast massive action.

Feel overwhelmed?

Make sure to invest 10 minutes to write down your ideal lifestyle, as we know how easy it is to get side tracked. Simply take the time to write down your answers to a few questions:

1. What do you enjoy doing in the business?
2. What are your goals with your business? To create a huge property portfolio? To make money? To do both? To build a business that you can sell? They're your goals, so spend some time doing this. It will help you get a clearer picture on what direction you should take when you come to a crossroad in your business; use this as your north star to keep you on track to achieve your goals.
3. What are your deadlines? Set deadlines and stick to them. For

example, if you want to take a family vacation in three months, write it out and get specific. Where will you stay? How long will you be gone? How will you get there? What will you do when you get there?

4. Implement and enjoy the process. It's very exciting to be here with you right now and we are excited to hear your success story, make sure to get your FREE bonuses by going to www.101WaysToGetLeads.com/599 and enjoy the audio version with the authors Mark Evans, DM, and Jay Conrad Levinson.

This is an exciting time for you, so use that excitement to implement as fast as humanly possible. Enjoy the momentum!

Make sure to refer back to this book often and remember you can always be doing more and, while we all want it quicker, do one step at a time.

Congratulations on making it this far! Make sure to check out the About the Authors pages to see how to learn more in depth training; you'll be happy you did.

Stop reading now and go DO IT!

Sample Forms

Disclaimer: This material is for information and educational purposes only. This material does not constitute professional, commercial or technical advice and, www.101WaysToGetLeads.com nor any of its affiliates accept liability for any problems arising through negligence or for any other reason whatsoever. Although care is taken to provide accurate information, there cannot, of course, be any guarantee about the suitability, completeness or accuracy and www.101WaysToGetLeads.com does not accept responsibility for the content of that material.

Assignment Form

______________assigns to _________________the Purchase Contract and/or Letter of Intent for the property located at:

__________________.

The original purchase contract is between ___________ and _________________, dated ____________. The contract is being assigned for the amount of $_______.

Upon execution of this assignment Agreement, New Buyer (Assignee) agrees to pay Original Buyer (Assignor) 100% of the above referenced option fee in the amount of
$______. New Buyer (Assignee) accepts all rights, obligations, and responsibilities of purchase contract executed by Original Buyer (Assignor) and the Seller of said property.

Original Buyer: ___________________________________
Date: ____
(Assignor – ______________________________)

New Buyer: ______________________________________
Date: ____
(Assignee – ______________________________)

Letter Of Intent

I am the owner of real estate located at _______________. It is my intent to enter into an agreement with (hereinafter referred to as "Buyer"), on the following terms:

1. I will sign an Option agreement and related documents giving Buyer the legal right to lease and/or buy my property.

2. Sales price to be $________.

3. Length of time for Buyer to exercise Option to be _____.

4. Buyer has the right to lease my property for the monthly amount of $_________.

5. Seller will prepare all documents at his/her expense to finalize this transaction.

6. I understand it is Buyer's intention to find a Lease Option Tenant to occupy this property and assign the rights to lease and/or purchase the property for a fee.

7. I agree to allow Buyer to put a sign in the yard, and advertise the property for sale.

This is a Letter Of Intent and is not binding. If these terms are acceptable to Buyer, he/she will prepare documents that are legally binding to be signed by the parties.

Signed this _____day of _____________, 20____.

Seller ______________________________

Buyer _______________________________

Option to Purchase

THIS AGREEMENT made this_____day of _______, 20__, between, ___________________, (collectively referred to as Optionor), and _______, (collectively referred
to as Optionee).

IN CONSIDERATION of the Optionee's payment of $____, the Optionor gives to Optionee the exclusive option, right and privilege of purchasing certain in real property located in the City of _____, County of ____, and State of ______, described as:

[Insert legal description]

Property Address: ___________________________

This option is subject to the following terms and conditions:

1) Optionor grants Optionee the exclusive right to exercise this option for a period commencing on the ____day of ___, and terminating at 11:59 p.m. on the ___ day of _______________________________, 20__.

2) The purchase price of the property will be $_______.

3) Notice of election to Purchase shall be given by Optionee in writing, and by first class mail, addressed to Optionor, at:
____.

4) The option consideration is for the sole purpose of granting the Optionee the exclusive right to purchase the subject property at the stated price and terms.

5) This option to purchase shall apply to and bind the heirs, executors, and administrator of the respective parties.

6) If the option is exercised, the related sale will be governed by a separate purchase contract executed by the parties concurrent with this Option.

7) Optionee has the right to multiple-list, advertise, rent or resell this property before or during this option period. In addition, Optionee has the right to freely assign this Option to a third party.

8) Time is of the essence in this agreement.

** Please let your local notary complete this page for you – it must be signed in their presence **

The parties have executed this agreement on the date first above written.

Optionor(s):	Optionee(s):
________________	________________
________________	________________

STATE OF ________)
) SS.
COUNTY OF __________)

The foregoing instrument was acknowledged before me this ____________________________20___________
by____________________.

REAL ESTATE PURCHASE CONTRACT

Dated this ___ day of _____, 20__, _______ (hereinafter "Buyer") and __________ (hereinafter "Seller") hereby enter into this contract for the sale of property located at: ____________________.

1. Purchase Price. The purchase price paid by Buyer in U.S. funds will be in the amount of $______.

2. Terms. ________________________________

(none if nothing inserted)

3. Contingencies.

A) Environmental Inspection: (This paragraph not applicable if number of days not inserted.) Within ___ days after the acceptance hereof, Seller agrees to permit the Buyer, Buyer's lender, and the qualified, professional environmental consultant of either of them to enter the premises to conduct, at the expense of the Buyer, an environmental site assessment. Buyer agrees to indemnify and hold Seller harmless from any injury or damage caused by such inspection. If such assessment is obtained and the consultant recommends further inspection to determine the extent of suspected contamination or recommends remedial action, the buyer, at Buyer's option may notify the Seller in writing, within the above specified period, that the contract is null and voice.

B) Property Inspection: (This paragraph not applicable if number of days is not inserted.) Buyer, at Buyer's expense, shall have __ days after the acceptance hereof to have the property and all improvement, fixtures, and equipment inspected. Seller shall cooperate in making the property reasonably available for such inspection(s). Buyer agrees to indemnify and hold Seller harmless from any injury or damage caused by such inspection(s). If Buyer is not satisfied with the condition of the property as disclosed by such inspection(s), Buyer may terminate this contract by delivering written notice of such termination to Seller within the time frame set forth in this paragraph.

C) Other Contingencies: ____________________

____

____

4. Title Insurance. Title insurance, if any will be paid by Buyer at Buyer's expense.

5. Taxes. Taxes will be pro-rated to the date of sale and Buyer will be given a credit at closing for any and all unpaid real estate taxes together with any and all penalties and interest.

6. Deed. Seller will provide marketable title via a general warranty deed with release of title to Buyer or Buyer's designee free and clear of all liens unless otherwise noticed (none if nothing inserted):

___________________________.

7. Legal representation. Both parties have had an opportunity to seek legal counsel to advise them in this transaction.

8. Broker representation. Both parties warrant that they

are not represented in this transaction by a licensed real estate broker or agent and no funds from this sale will be paid to a licensed real estate broker or agent.

9. Closing date. The parties agree that the closing will take place on or before the __ day of ____, 20__ at a title company of the Buyer's choosing. Buyer shall receive possession at closing.

10. Fixtures. This sale shall include any and all fixtures to the property including but not limited to: heating and air conditioning equipment, built-in appliances, curtains and curtain rods, attached carpeting, attached mirrors and lights, screens and storm doors/windows, garage door openers, TV reception systems, outbuildings and all exterior plants and trees except as follows (none if nothing inserted): _______
____________________________.

11. Other. All representations and warranties of the parties are set forth in this contract and shall survive the closing. There are no representations, or agreements of the parties that have not been incorporated into this agreement.

12. Successors. This agreement and all provisions hereof shall be binding upon and inure to the benefit of the parties hereto and their respective heirs, executors, administrators, legal representatives, successors and permitted assigns.

13. Risk of Loss. Seller bears the risk of loss to the property up to the time of closing. In the event that the property has incurred damage in the amount of $5,000 or

more, the Buyer may cancel this contract within 7 days of receiving written notice of the damage from Seller.

Signed on the date first written above.

________________________ ________________________

BUYER SELLER

BUYER NOTICE OF TERMINATION OF THE CONTRACT*

Premises Address:

____

Seller:

____

Buyer:

____

Accepted Contract Date: ____________________

The Buyer is terminating the Real Estate Purchase Contract for the following reason:

____ Lender's Pre-Approval cannot be taken to completion

____ Lender's Written Loan Commitment cannot be taken to completion

____ Inspections and Tests: The Buyer has the right to have inspections and tests of the premises and to give this notice on or before ______________.

The undersigned Buyer notifies the Seller that the Buyer is not, in good faith, satisfied with the condition of the premises because of unsatisfactory conditions and hereby terminates the Real Estate Purchase Contract.

____ Damage or Destruction of Premises

____Other:

____
____
____

The Buyer requests the return of any/all of the Buyer's Earnest Money Deposit within 7 days of the date of this letter.

Buyer: __________________________________
Buyer: __________________________________
Date: __________________________________

*It is recommended that all parties be represented by Legal Counsel.

ASSIGNMENT FORM
(Cash Transaction)

_____________ assigns to ___________ the Purchase Contract and/or Letter of Intent for the property located at: ________________________.

The original purchase contract is between ________ and ___________, and is dated __________. The contract is being assigned for the amount of $______.

Upon execution of this assignment Agreement, New Buyer (Assignee) agrees to pay Original Buyer (Assignor) 100% of the above referenced assignment fee in the amount of $________.

This assignment fee is non-refundable and represents both parties entering into a legal, binding contract. By signing below, New Buyer (Assignee) accepts all rights, obligations, and responsibilities of the Purchase Contract executed by Original Buyer (Assignor) and the Seller of said property.

Original Buyer: _________________ Date: ______
(Assignor—please print name: ________________)

New Buyer: ____________________Date: ______
(Assignee—please print name: ________________)

Script for We Buy Guys & Other Investors

The idea is to call these guys up to see what they have going on and to see if they will be valuable additions to your Power Team…and you to theirs. Respect their time and keep the calls short and sweet. You don't need but 3-5 minutes of their time to really get a feel for what they're looking for and how you can help each other, so don't get caught up in chit chat – there's money to be made!
Hello. I'm calling about your:
a) ad in the paper
b) ad I saw on the www.______.com website
c) sign you had posted saying you buy houses
d) etc.

I was wondering if you could fax me your current property listings and add me to your distribution list for when you get new ones in? Here's my contact info.

Please be sure to include as much detail about the properties as you can:
a) beds / baths / square footage / address / asking price, etc.

If you don't mind, do you have a few minutes to talk to me about the kind of investing that YOU do so that I can keep you in mid when I run across deals?

Yes? Great…<Take them through the Investor Profile.>

What type of properties are you looking for?

- Single family homes?
- Multiple family homes (2-4 units)?
- Commercial properties?

- An apartment complex?

What category would you way you are in at this time?
- Beginner?
- Intermediate?
- Experienced?

What exit strategy do you do most of?
- I hold and keep for long-term rentals.
- Quick flip.
- Rehab and resale on the retail market.
- Rehab and resale on the investor market (turnkey).

What would you say is the biggest thing in your business that you want more of?
- Buyer leads.
- Seller leads.
- More networking with like-minded investors.
- Access to money to do more deals.

When you are presented a deal, how long does it take you to make a decision on moving forward?
- Immediately.
- Within 24 hours.
- 24-48 hours.
- 48 hours or more.

How quickly are you looking to purchase a property?
- ASAP.
- Within 30 days.
- Not ready to buy yet. Still learning the ropes.

What is your #1 method to purchase deals at this time?
- Cash?
- Financing?
- Hard money?

- Owner financing?
- No money at all; I'm going to wholesale to another buyer.

What would you say is the biggest obstacle you face in your real estate business at this time?

Can you paint a picture for me of the best scenario of a deal you would like me to bring to you?

When I bring you a deal, how fast can you typically close?

Do you fund your deals yourself or do you have cash partners?

****

You should also take a minute to ask them about their knowledge of "Subject To" investing. No matter what their response, you need to tell them to get over to this awesome website to get their complete, free eCourse on how to investing using the Sub-2 Magic Method.

Tell them you'll email them the link as soon as you get off the phone, and they better hurry over and get their download because you're not too sure how much longer the course is going to be free, so they don't want to miss out. Remember, if they buy the upgrade package for $97, we'll pay you $48.50!

Your affiliate link is: ___________________________
(log into your account at www.sub2magic.com/login.php to get this off of your home page)

This book is happy to support charities such as The Caring House Project Foundation and the Get Kids Fishing Foundation.

The Caring House Project Foundation

It was the Gospel of Luke that taught me:

"Much will be required of the person entrusted with much, and still more demanded of the person entrusted with more."

In 1998, my wife, Nilsa, and I founded the Caring House Project Foundation. Our primary objective is to provide housing, food, water, medical support and opportunity for the desperately homeless around the world, particularly in South America, the Caribbean, Indonesia, and here in the United States of America.

Think of the deep satisfaction experienced when seeing a self-sufficient village literally rise up out of the ground.

Contemplate the incredible impact that can be made on thousands and thousands of lives not just for today, but for generations.

This process is part of my business plan, my responsibility to steward the blessings God has entrusted with me.

Won't you join us by getting involved today?

Feel The Tap...

Frank McKinney

Learn more by going to:
www.Frank-McKinney.com/caring_project.aspx

Get Kids Fishing Charity

Mission statement: Get Kids Fishing Foundation, USA™ is a not-for-profit organization dedicated to being active in our community, giving our youth the knowledge and tools to enjoy the sport of fishing and teaching them how to respect and protect the great outdoors.

"The GKF^2 goal is to make every child's fishing dream come true. We accomplish this exciting adventure threw education, encouragement, and life changing outdoor experiences. So, please get on board and be part of the team that will help GKF^2 make great fishing dreams come true."

Dave Dayton, Founder of GKF^2
www.GetKidsFishing.org

About the Authors

Jay Conrad Levinson is the author of the best-selling marketing series in history, *Guerrilla Marketing*, plus 59 other business books. His books have sold more than 21-million copies worldwide. His guerrilla concepts have influenced marketing so much that his books appear in 62 languages and are required reading in MBA programs across the globe.

He was born in Detroit, raised in Chicago, and graduated from the University of Colorado. His studies in Psychology led him to advertising agencies, including a Directorship at Leo Burnett in London, where he served as Creative Director. Upon his return to the US, he joined J. Walter Thompson as Senior VP. Jay created and taught guerrilla marketing for ten years at the extension division of the University of California in Berkeley.

A winner of first prizes in all the media, he has been part of the creative teams that made household names of The Marlboro Man, The Pillsbury Doughboy, Allstate's good hands, United's friendly skies, Sears' Diehard battery, Morris the Cat, Mr. Clean, Tony the Tiger, and the Jolly Green Giant.

Today, *Guerrilla Marketing* is most the powerful brand in the history of marketing, listed among the 100 best business books ever written, a popular website at www.gmarketing.com, and powers The Guerrilla Marketing Association, a support system for small business.

After living in the San Francisco Bay Area for 35 years, Jay and Jeannie Levinson sold their home, bought an RV, towed a Jeep, and ended up, six years later, at their lakefront home outside Orlando, Florida, and close to their 26 grandchildren—their own personal Disney World. Nobody on earth is as qualified to write about Guerrilla Marketing than the Father of Guerrilla Marketing, Jay Conrad Levinson.

Mark Evans, DM, is a full-time world traveler and full-time virtual real estate investor. He is a master at creating multiple streams of income and is a life-long student of marketing. As such, he has turned his attention toward reaching out to others to teach them how to live life on their terms.

Mark has developed many groundbreaking online systems and best-selling real estate products. These online tools allow investors to easily create multiple streams of income online in their sleep. Not only is Mark a real estate investor but he has subsequently become a successful real estate investing coach, and has students all around the world. He gets excited about helping others who are ready and willing to help themselves! His willingness to help is more than just words—Mark offers simple but powerful instruction, guidance and direction through his many programs.

This three-time best-selling author (with many more to come) has a passion and a zest for life that is infectious. This zeal for life and reaching out is reflected in the fact that he donates book sale percentages to many well-deserving charitable foundations. These philanthropic endeavors help those less fortunate. Says Mark, "We can always do more by helping others to achieve their goals."

By achieving all of this (and more!), Mark Evans, DM, truly does live up to his title of Deal Maker.

Contacting the Author

Mark Evans DM has a busy schedule—working his real estate investing business and traveling across the world with his family…all while continuing to strive for excellence in business as well in helping his students propel forward to become more profitable, all through using systems.

However, he is always looking for opportunities to help those individuals who understand that success is a lifestyle. Those who are committed to achieving their goals may have the chance to take advantage of Mark's coaching, books, teleseminars, and live workshops. Please contact Mark's office at the web address below to see if you qualify for his available programs.

Mark Evans DM may also be available for speaking and seminar engagements, mentoring, consulting, marketing, and interviews, both for TV and radio.

To contact Mark Evans DM directly, go to www.MarkEvansDM.com

Gift Certificate

$599 Value

To: You the Reader

From: Guerrilla Marketing for Real Estate Investors

Good For: Waiver of the $599 set up fee when getting your fully automated Squeeze pages with bonuses for **FREE**

To Redeem This Certificate Please Visit:

www.101WaysToGetLeads.com/599

This Certificate Holds No Cash Value.

6735772R0

Made in the USA
Lexington, KY
16 September 2010